HOPE

When Everything Seems Hopeless

THOMAS P. DOOLEY, PH.D.

HOPE

When Everything Seems Hopeless

Thomas P. Dooley, Ph.D.

I don't see the point of prosperity & wellbeing
in life y All it does is distract you from
Jesus / x .

Mall Publishing Co.

THE PRINTED WORD THE PLANTED SEED

HIGHLAND PARK, ILLINOIS

Cover Design and Text Design by Marlon B. Villadiego

ISBN: 1-934165-20-4

Printed in the United States of America

Published by:
Mall Publishing
641 Homewood Avenue
Highland Park, Illinois 60035
1.877.203.2453

For licensing / copyright information, for additional copies or for use in specialized settings contact:

Path Clearer, Inc.
PO Box 661466
Birmingham, Alabama
35266-1466 USA
info@pathclearer.com
www.pathclearer.com
www.tomdooley.org

—

ENDORSEMENTS

Tom Dooley is not only a thinker, but a deep thinker. And as one would expect of him, this book is not a river to wade across, but one whose current will lift your feet from the bottom and challenge you to swim. Believe me, in a day when the lamp of hope has gone out in many places, it is a welcome change to see a new light in the dark. *Hope When Everything Seems Hopeless* is that kind of book. The river may be turbulent, but the light on the other side is bright. Just minutes before picking up this manuscript I read another which predicted nothing but despair and gloom. Then, unexpectedly, "Hope" came – strong, assuring, faith-filled and confident. Read it! You need it!

Charles Carrin

Six Decades of Ministry as Pastor, Author, and Conference Speaker
(Boynton Beach, Florida)

For many people today, life has become hopeless. That's why Dr. Tom Dooley's book on hope carries the promise of making a difference in the lives of so many. Writing from a biblical worldview, using vivid illustrations and with the perspective of an encourager, Tom clarifies the often misunderstood "I hope so" mindset of those who fail to understand the true nature of this vital quality. *Hope When Everything Seems Hopeless* is a book that will infuse you with an understanding of hope that will enable you to choose hope, since *"the mind is the major battleground in the struggle against hopelessness."* Ultimately it will point you to Jesus, Whose *"hope is superior to any we can muster."*

Dr. Don Hawkins

President of Southeastern Bible College, Author,
Host of *Life Perspectives* Radio
(Birmingham, Alabama)

Hope is linked with your emotions. Without hope, you have no expectation and you lose sight of the road ahead. One of the greatest demonic forces that we must battle is disappointment which leads to hope deferred which leads to sickness and infirmity. Tom Dooley brings light into darkness that will turn your weeping into laughter. Once you embrace hope, resurrection power follows. *Hope When Everything Seems Hopeless* will lead you into a new expressed manifestation of God's power in your life.

Chuck D. Pierce
President of Glory of Zion International Ministries,
Harvest Watchman of Global Harvest Ministries, Author

The world we live in is like a stinking trash dump. Sometimes, we are like Mr. Boular having all the reasons to act as defeated in view of being handicapped. But, hope sees beyond circumstances, beyond the "now". Hope is looking into the future. Through this wonderful book, Dr. Thomas Dooley is a hope-giver to a hopeless world.

Peter Dugulescu
Pastor, Author,
Former Member of the Parliament of Romania
(Timisoara, Romania), deceased January 3, 2008

This book is a virtual treasure chest of remarkable teachings and illustrations that will inspire hope for those in the pit of despair and hopelessness. Tom Dooley reveals how to reach out and grasp the hand of the One who is more than able, and willing, to lift, to heal, and to restore.

David Ravenhill
Author & Itinerant Teacher
(Lindale, Texas)

"There will be signs in the sun, moon and stars. On the earth, nations will be in anguish and perplexity at the roaring and tossing of the sea. Men will faint from terror, apprehensive of what is coming on the world, for the heavenly bodies will be shaken" (Luke 21:25-6). One need but marginal discernment to realize that the fulfillment of this excerpt of scripture is now lapping at our feet—not unlike a very subtle, incoming tide. In an hour when anxiety medication sales are fueling the pharmaceutical industry to the tune of *billions* of dollars per year, hope stands ready to guide us through the darkest mire. But hope is a choice. Tom Dooley has penned a beautiful invitation to embrace hope as the quarterdeck upon which we may navigate the worst of storms ahead.

David Davenport
Prophetic Pastor & Bi-vocational Minister,
MorningStar Fellowship of Ministries
(Somerville, Ohio)

Hope When Everything Seems Hopeless communicates the message of hope in a way that is both practical and life-giving. But, this book is more than just great ideas. You get years of experience of a man who needed hope himself and lived out these principles. Tom is a gift to the Kingdom and so is this book! Read it and apply it, and you'll discover that hope can change everything.

Chris Hodges
Pastor, Church of the Highlands
(Birmingham, Alabama)

Mankind is in an epidemic of hopelessness because he has chosen to ignore and reject the only sure cure for it, Jesus, The Messiah, the Son of God. Tom's book will encourage you to discover and know that the foundation of hope in Christ can lead to a life of faith and victory in a defeated and despairing world.

Dee Baxter
President of Baxter Bible Ministries, Inc.
(La Fayette, Georgia)

—

Tom Dooley writes on the forgotten virtue of the Christian trinity of eternal values - *hope*. Christian hope is not a wishfulness for change, but is an anchor of certainty that will keep the soul. This book records testimonies and comments that will prove inspirational for those who find themselves in hopeless situations. Apart from hope, Tom writes in a challenging and insightful way.

Dr. David Elms
Pastor of Kingsway Christian Fellowship
(Liverpool, England)

When I first read my friend's new book title my spirit was stirred, because encouragement is a core area of ministry in my own life. As ministers we carry the responsibility to show others how to find hope and to turn hopeless situations around into breakthroughs. Dr. Dooley has provided many remarkable stories of breakthroughs that he has gathered from his experiences and travels among the nations. This book will give hope to many.

Brown Oyitso
Provincial Pastor and International Church Planter of
The Redeemed Christian Church of God
(Lagos, Nigeria)

Hope is such a powerful divine energy that keeps us motivated until we possess the full inheritance. It is truly a divine power within us working towards the fulfillment of every God-given goal. This book by my friend, Tom Dooley, will bless a lot of people.

Derek Kuhn
Pastor of Grace Covenant Church, Singer-Songwriter
(Chicago, Illinois)

Dr. Dooley holistically elaborates on hope. Firstly, he defines hope and then tells of hope's relation to faith. The book is also filled with examples of hope from the Bible, world history, and personal examples. As a prophet, he elaborates on hope and hopelessness in the context of present society. Dr. Dooley's goal is to progressively take the reader *"out of the pit of the impossible into the progressively higher realms of the possible, the probable, and the prophetic."* It will give practical hope and wisdom to the readers.

Dr. Liu
Community development leader
(China)

This "dealer in hope" shares it with his readers - explaining hope in a Biblical and practical way, and pointing towards the One and only, Who is able to give it, sustain it, and make it happen! Read it and keep hoping!

Nicu Gramesc
President of Christ for Romania Christian Center, Pastor of St. Andrew Church
(Suceava, Romania)

FOREWORD

In the fall of 2003, several dozen people gathered at Tom Dooley's home for an enlightened evening of Bible study. This was my first encounter with a vibrant personality, whose selfless devotion to the call of Christ has taken him around the world, proclaiming truth and helping people. I have had the privilege of walking with Dr. Dooley and accompanying him on several ministry venues on the continents of Europe and Asia. These journeys have been adventures with unusual signs and wonders, as well as down-to-earth "helps" that have revealed Jesus to needy people.

There are unique times in history when all the lines intersect to form a special moment for mankind. It is during those days that God raises up His prophets to articulate His desires and plans for a generation. I believe that we are in such a time, and Dr. Tom Dooley is such a voice. In his first book, *Praying Faith*, Tom introduced a living word that was designed to help God's people hear the voice of the Good Shepherd. Now, with his second book, *Hope When Everything Seems Hopeless*, a timely word is extended to give courage to the "little flock" so they may continue on and inherit the Kingdom.

Tom Dooley is at the right place and is at the right time to make a significant difference for those who hear. He is at the right place in his walk with God. Having truly been born again, he has been in the loving and faithful hands of our Father. It is in this place that he has learned humility and the desire to do justly and to walk uprightly. Tom's devotion to his lovely wife, Laura, and their four children is indeed an expression of covenant and this loyalty cries out the word – integrity. I have witnessed firsthand his painfully honest associations with business and ministry associates alike. This is where honesty meets the road, and in all of these relationships Tom has stood tall and firm. I appreciate this quality in any prophet with whom I choose to run. Dr. Dooley is also at the right time. This is proving to be an absolutely glorious time for believers in Jesus Christ. These are also times that try men's souls. His words of hope come from the crucible of life and are freely given to others so that they might enjoy life.

I hope you, the reader, will learn to love and appreciate the "life lessons" of this unique and gifted person, as I have as his colleague and friend. My prayer is that you will discover not just the message of the man, but the loving God that is behind the man.

Don Stewart
Bi-vocational Minister, Member of the Board of Path Clearer
(Hamilton, Alabama)

TABLE OF CONTENTS

ACKNOWLEDGEMENTS

I believe that there are three key components to a truly meaningful life – *faith, family, and friends*. Each of these represents a unique type of relationship.

Foremost of these, I am grateful to Jesus for giving to us His hope, a hope that is superior to any that we can muster. Within the incubator of hope, faith is birthed. But without hope, faith can never get a foothold in our lives.

I am grateful for the continuous support of my immediate family, including my loving wife, Laura, and our four precious children, Isaac, Catherine, Jeannette, and Thomas. They have sacrificed to allow me to become a blessing to others. Without their selfless love and support, it is doubtful that I would have much of merit worthy of writing. Each of them deserves credit and honor for their innumerable contributions to my life, and subsequently this project.

And finally, I am grateful to all of our numerous friends around the globe, who have been sources of encouragement. Some of their testimonies and endorsements are shared within this work. The Path Clearer ministry team and those who help us *Influence the Nations with Judeo-Christian Truth* has been a great encouragement. In particular I am grateful to one trusted friend in England, John Manwell. He was asked to contribute a solicited chapter on the theme of hope, in order to provide confirmation and additional insights on this timely topic.

For all of these precious relationships I give thanks to Yahweh - the Eternal God, the Holy Spirit, and the Creator-Son.

DEDICATION

This work is dedicated to the two other Thomas Dooley's in my family, my father and my youngest son. My father, Thomas E. Dooley, has been a hardworking farmer and laborer in Kansas. I recall from my youth his demonstrations of respect for the Almighty by kneeling at his bedside in prayer late at night after working at a grain elevator, and by taking our family of six children to attend church services every Sunday. His humor, hospitality, and kindness are well known in the Good Intent farming community. My youngest son, Thomas S. Dooley, is an intellectually gifted and compassionate young man. He has the ability to discern the depth of pain suffered by others, and has an uncommon awareness of the reality of the Spirit realm. In view of the challenges the two of them have faced in recent years, my father and my youngest son have both needed to embrace *hope when everything seems hopeless*. May the Lord bless them and keep them and cause His face to shine upon them and grant them peace! May His perfect will for each of them be fulfilled.

PART I
HOPE TO THE RESCUE

This book was written especially for hurting individuals, those who are buried under the snowdrift of hopelessness and left there as half-dead. May this book breathe a measure of *hope*, which is the bedrock upon which genuine *faith* is established. Without hope there can be no faith. And without faith, one cannot please God.

May each of us come to know the Almighty God and His provision at all times. We especially need Him during those discouraging seasons when we are in despair. May the precious Holy Spirit dwelling within us as Believers expand our eyes to see and our ears to hear what He desires. May the Creator give us His revelation of our intended purposes and destinies. May we see beyond our "today"!

This book was written with two biases, that of a Biblical worldview and that derived from the author's personal experiences and insights. It points in the direction of Jesus the Creator-Son, as the answer. Not one of many answers, but *The Answer*. Real hope should be anchored in a context of solid Biblical theology, and in particular in the essential reality of the resurrected Jesus. It is at the cross of Jesus where the power of hope was released in full measure on the earth.

This book reflects the experiences and limited understanding of the author. In as much as the author is human and is prone to error, please be a good *Berean* and check within the Scriptures if the conclusions resonate with God-inspired Truth. Eat the chicken, but spit out the bones.

This book is meant to stir our hearts when the tide is slipping away. May the examples of other individuals who have prevailed while in their own dark valleys give you the boost necessary to see you through another day during your own *season of shaking*.

1
LIGHT PIERCING THE DARKNESS

*"The people living in darkness have seen a great light; on those living
in the land of the shadow of death a light has dawned."*

~ Isaiah 9:2; Matthew 4:16

In the early 20th century in the Kansas town of Atchison, a deaf
mute named William Boular stood out from his contemporaries as
a man worthy of distinction and honor. However, he wasn't a doctor,
a lawyer, or a politician. Mr. Boular had lost his hearing at the age of
four due to spinal meningitis, resulting in him being referred to by the
denigrating nickname "Deafy". Though life had dealt him an apparent
"bad hand", he was an accomplished bricklayer and also racked pool
balls for the patrons of a local pool hall.

Prior to William's death in 1953, this hardworking stout laborer was
familiar to my father, Tom, and to my father's two older brothers, Bill and
Joe. I wasn't born for another six years, and was unfortunately too late to
ever encounter Mr. Boular. But, I wish I had met him for the remarkable
stories told and recorded about him.

What sets Mr. Boular apart from others are two noteworthy distinctions.
In one particular eight-hour workday he *alone* laid 46,000 individual bricks
to pave a portion of Atchison's historic brick streets, some of which
survive to this day. Many visitors who come to my hometown drive over
the "talking" paved brick streets to learn of the town's history, including
visiting the home of Amelia Earhart, the famous trans-oceanic aviatrix.
William Boular's amazing accomplishment for a deaf-mute laborer earned
him a distinction in *Ripley's Believe it or Not* in 1933. But, even more striking

is the fact that this remarkable *feat* of hard labor was accomplished without any literal *feet!* Due to his childhood hearing loss, Mr. Boular had been run over by a train at the age of twelve and lost both of his lower legs in the tragic accident.

William Boular epitomizes the hope of a determined optimist, one who is not weighed down mentally by the burden of his present unfortunate circumstances. He made lemonade out of his lemon, and lived life to the full. He refused to pout and mope around as a handicapped man. He could have resigned to the possibility that he would not be effective as a worker and thus become a handicapped beggar by default. But, he had a positive attitude based in hope. Mr. Boular used his remaining physical skills and determination to realize a productive life. His "unfortunate" shortened legs became an "asset" in view of his optimistic outlook, as his perspective focused on the ground nearby as a street bricklayer. His unfortunate weakness became his strength. Being close to the ground gave him an advantage, but only after he had conquered his own mental perspective. He was an amputee lacking feet, yet he was far from defeated!

For many of us, we can relate well to hardships, many of which have surrounded us by no fault of our own. Hardships come in many forms – death, disease, unemployment, accusation, poverty, physical and verbal abuse, abandonment, crime, litigation, loss of a business, and the lack of "good things" enjoyed by others. There is no lack of horrible circumstances or situations in the world. Even Jesus said, *"I have told you these things, so that in me you may have peace. In this world you will have trouble. But take heart! I have overcome the world."* (John 16:33). Another translation reads, *"In this world you shall have tribulation."* Friends, we're not in paradise yet. We haven't arrived in the land of constant glory. Our earthly existence is fraught with many difficulties.

Our difficult circumstances often appear to be set in granite. We believe that we're powerless to change them at that juncture. However, we can do one thing. We can change the thoughts within our minds. We can voluntarily adopt an attitude of *hope.* This precious commodity is the on-ramp to the highway to recovery from the pit of despair. The Lord can lift you up from your pit and set your feet firmly upon the Rock.

Our minds have the freedom to embrace hope or to abandon it. It is our choice. The poet Oscar Wilde commented that, *"We are all in the gutter, but some of us are looking at the stars."* We will remain downtrodden until we take captive the thoughts of the mind that would seek to limit us and shackle us to the pain. The mind is the major battleground in the struggle against hopelessness. But, we can choose what our minds dwell upon. My good friend Howard Morgan encourages us to, *"Think about what you think about."* Simple, yet profound. We are not required to dwell upon the obstacles. Rather, we make a choice.

TRANSFORMING A HOPELESS SITUATION IN NIGERIA

During my first ministry trip to Lagos, Nigeria in 2001, I was traveling with a group of leaders of the Redeemed Christian Church of God. We traveled in several cars in a caravan to visit with many local RCCG pastors around Lagos. We stopped and prayed briefly with the local leaders at each site and then drove on to the next location.

One stop in particular will forever be recalled with fondness. Two men had begun a new congregation. They were evangelist-pastors "planting" a church in this community. They desired to build a facility for their new congregation. However, they had a problem. They didn't have much money. But, they had something more precious than money.

When we arrived we were escorted into the middle of many acres of filth and rubbish several feet deep. We were standing in the middle of a trash dump. Not exactly a Western World type of a landfill created by a bulldozer. It was just rubbish on top of the earth. In the center of this trash-filled area was approximately one acre that had been cleared of all rubbish down to plain dirt. Birds and stray animals rummaged through the stinking mess surrounding it. Sitting nearby among the trash were several rough looking thugs, who made mocking comments toward us from a distance. They seemed to be mimicking demonic manifestations to challenge our presence in the forsaken territory in which they were squatters without legitimate entitlement. Initially I was a bit confused, in part due to jetlag from the day and a half of travel to get there from the United States. But, I had a hard time for a minute comprehending why we had stopped our caravan of vehicles to walk into the middle of such a depressing location. I was thinking to myself, *"What are we doing here?"*

These two optimistic Nigerian church planters were effervescent with hope that produced a tangible and infectious faith in God. They believed that God Almighty would use *this* site to build their new facility! Yes, right there in the middle of a West African trash dump. I could barely believe my eyes at first thought of this scenario. I thought, *"Who in their right mind would want to be part of a congregation in the middle of a smelly trash dump?"* I was dumbfounded. However, the hope expressed by these two Nigerian ministers so impressed all of us on the site visit team.

I asked the two men why they had chosen this particular site. They replied that since this was a trash dump the price would be a bargain for this first parcel of land, because no one would really want it while it was surrounded by garbage. Then, once they possessed this first parcel and started to build, they could push back the *darkness* of the evil spiritual climate of that area. They intended to continue to expand progressively into other adjacent sections of this under-valued property. These two disciples of Jesus wanted a blessing, so we joyfully prayed down God's favor upon their faith-filled project of land reclamation.

To an affluent American or European this strategy might seem ridiculous. But, it was profoundly brilliant from a Kingdom of God perspective. It would kill two birds with one stone; the filth would be destroyed and a new wholesome purpose would rise up. Darkness would be compelled to give way to light. What better way to maximize limited financial resources for a new congregation than to reclaim lost ground for use in the Kingdom. And, once completed, the project would undoubtedly be profoundly effective and beautiful. It would become a testimony of hope and redemption to be shared for years to come. The confident hope that gave rise to risk-taking belief in action by these two Nigerians was commendable.

A trash dump is a metaphor for a hopeless situation. But, once hope is stirred up the seemingly impossible then becomes possible. *"For nothing is impossible with God."* (Luke 1:37). But, those who lack hope will *never* initiate a walk down the path toward genuine faith. They'll just remain mired in the worthless debris and mud of their own trash dump. Real faith is defined in my book <u>Praying Faith</u> as *risk-taking belief in action*. Faith can never happen until after one feels the wind of hope lifting up the wings of faith. In order to do so, one must have the *eyes of faith* to see beyond the current negative circumstances that are recognized by our natural *eyes of sight*. Hope is where it all starts. Without hope one can never have any faith.

In Third World countries most individuals lack the privileges and comforts of the West. I've enjoyed many opportunities of traveling in some challenging poor areas of the world. For instance, the working poor of India are paid perhaps one or two dollars each day, while many Western business employees make that amount in minutes or if they're extremely affluent even in seconds. Yet, the laborers of India often have hope in spite of difficult circumstances. Some of them collect scraps of waste plastic for recycling for a few Rupies (i.e., a few pennies) per bundle. Others set up shop on a street corner to mend and polish shoes or to patch bicycle tires. Others carry pallets of bricks on their heads or backs to a construction site like small beasts of burden. Others use handmade brooms to sweep a storefront. Others collect dried manure for use as cooking fuel. The desire to survive and thrive will force one to see opportunities overlooked or concealed from the haughty eyes of the more affluent.

If you have never traveled in a Third World country, plan to do so at least once in your lifetime. Look for the hope and ingenuity of the local people. Look in their eyes and you'll likely see more contentment, virtue, and optimism than in the eyes of millionaires in the West, who are occupied with so many distractions.

While visiting Ibadan, Nigeria I noticed many industrious merchants selling goods along the streets. They carried their wares into the congested streets to sell to people waiting in cars that were temporarily stalled in traffic. They brought to the car windows handicrafts, newspapers, plastic pouches of drinking water, candies, and rats. Yes, dead rats hanging upside down by their dead tails! I could barely believe my eyes at that scene. I asked my friend Samuel Sorinmade, *"Why would anyone sell a dead rat?"* Samuel chuckled and replied, *"Oh, they're not selling rats. They're using the dead carcasses to demonstrate that their rat poison is effective!"* I stood corrected and humbled, while laughing at my misunderstanding. Come to think of it, I don't know many Westerners who would hold a dead rat by the tail, just to make a meager living on the streets.

WHAT IS HOPE?

Hope is defined in Webster's Dictionary as either a verb or noun as *"to cherish a desire with expectation of fulfillment; to long for with expectation of obtainment; to expect with desire; desire accompanied by expectation of or belief in fulfillment"*. Hopelessness is its antithesis, meaning *"having no expectation of good or success; despairing; not susceptible to remedy or cure; incapable of solution, management, or accomplishment"*. I view hope as *mental optimism in spite of obstacles or circumstances.* A related manifestation is the *anticipation of future fulfillment of a desire.* No single definition fully captures the intended manifold meanings of this virtue. For an overview of the various Hebrew and Greek terms used in the Bible for hope, please read Never Give Up by Dr. Don Hawkins.

Hope is not only a human virtue, but it is established as one of the cardinal spiritual virtues – faith, hope, and love that are recorded in the Scriptures (see I Corinthians 13:13). Unfortunately, often people when encountering a difficult situation say the simple remark, *"I hope so…"*, when in fact they really mean the exact opposite. They really have doubt that it will ever be accomplished. Ironically this phrase isn't really about hope; this expression is about not having hope. The misuse of the term "hope" in this often quoted phrase has eroded and neutered the intended meaning of genuine hope.

Though it might appear otherwise, hope is *not* defined by our circumstances. But, hope is certainly tested by them. Hope is defined by our attitude regardless of the circumstances and obstacles we are facing. Hope is volitional. It is a mindset engaged with a view to recognize the positive possibilities that might lie ahead. Our mental choices to embrace hope can only be made by us. No one else can make it for us. We all appreciate encouragement when we're in a valley. But, you or I alone choose whether we embrace hope or not…and we do so as an individual. Hope can be stirred by external words of encouragement and cheerleading from others. But, we must ultimately internalize hope as an expression of our own thoughts and spirits.

Our hope as believers is ultimately found in Jesus, the Creator-Son. Paul said, *"Who shall separate us from the love of Christ? Shall trouble or hardship or persecution or famine or nakedness or danger or sword?…For I am convinced that neither death nor life, neither angels nor demons, neither the present nor the future, nor any powers, neither height nor depth, nor anything else in all creation, will be able to separate us from the love of God that is in Christ Jesus our Lord."* (Romans 8:35, 38-39). Circumstances or the actions of others cannot remove us from His love. The source of our hope remains secure. None can take us from the palm of His hand.

But, I do see one caveat. We can do it by ourselves. We can choose to fan the flames of hope while enduring a seemingly hopeless situation, or we can choose to give up. It is up to us alone to determine what we'll think and believe.

There is a very close relationship between hope and faith. Both anticipate the future, and both are tested by adversity. Hope is at the core of faith. Paul wrote to the Roman believers, *"We know that the whole creation has been groaning as in the pains of childbirth right up to the present time. Not only so, but we ourselves, who have the firstfruits of the Spirit, groan inwardly as we wait eagerly for our adoption as sons, the redemption of our bodies. For in this hope we were saved. But hope that is seen is no hope at all. Who hopes for what he already has? But if we hope for what we do not yet have, we wait for it patiently."* (Romans 8:22-24). Hope only operates when the object of desire has yet to be received. Hope speaks of the future, but appropriates belief for today. Hope works only in advance. It waits to receive the outcome. *"…but those who hope in the Lord will renew their strength. They will soar on wings like eagles; they will run and not grow weary, they will walk and not be faint."* (Isaiah 40:31). Another translation says, *"those who wait upon the Lord"*.

Hope determines whether you dwell *in* the valley of the shadow of death or you pass *through* it! (see Psalm 23). I'm especially fond of Jesus' own encouragement toward us, *"Come to me, all who are weary and burdened, and I will give you rest. Take my yoke upon you and learn from me, for I am gentle and humble in heart, and you will find rest for your souls. For my yoke is easy and my burden is light."* (Matt. 11:28-30). In order to pass through the tests of difficult circumstances, as believers we benefit when we realize the truth of these words. He offers rest as we become co-laborers in the same yoke that symbolizes a pair of oxen working side-by-side. Imagine a wooden curved beam resting upon your shoulders, and adjacent to you is Jesus holding up the other half. The Holy Spirit is described in Greek as the *parakletos*, meaning the one standing beside you as your counselor. The key is that you two are mutually pulling the same load. We as individuals don't need to bear all of the weight of a burden alone. We just need to do two things. We must remove any self-imposed burden that He never intended for us to carry, and we must only pick up the burdens on His agenda. When we're unencumbered of unnecessary weights and are only working toward His will, then we'll find productive fellowship with Him as one of His co-laborers. Even in the midst of darkness His yoke is easy and His burden is light. Note that Jesus did not say that He would remove *all* burdens. Some burdens will remain upon our shoulders. However, He said He would lighten our burdens. And, who knows better what burdens we can handle than the Creator-Son.

The prophet Isaiah refers to men like blades of grass. *"Their people, drained of power, are dismayed and put to shame. They are like tender green shoots, like grass sprouting on the roof, scorched before it grows up."* (Isaiah 37:27). *"… All men are like grass, and all their glory is like the flowers of the field. The grass withers and the flowers fall, because the breath of the Lord blows on them. Surely the people are grass. The grass withers and the flowers fall, but the word of our God stands forever."* (Isaiah 40:6-8).

Blades of grass are short-lived and lacking in strength. Compare a blade of grass to a giant cypress tree and you'll note how susceptible a stem of grass is to wind, water, and being trampled upon. In this metaphor the proud man stands tall, whereas the humble are bowed low (i.e., wilting due to limited water). *"A bruised reed he will not break, and a smoldering wick he will not snuff out. In faithfulness he will bring forth justice: he will not falter or be discouraged till he establishes justice on the earth. In his law the islands will put their hope."* (Isaiah 42:3-4). God is opposed to the proud, but He gives grace to the humble. The good news is that a broken reed He will not crush! He will level every mountain of pride and elevate every valley of humility (see Isaiah 40:3-6). He is the defender of the downcast and the oppressed. If you are a broken reed today and lacking in hope, He desires to lift you up.

THE EYE IS THE LAMP OF THE BODY

The one who carries hope within becomes the source of light in the darkness. Often times we view Jesus (and the Holy Spirit) as primarily

—

external to our being. We see Him as a lighthouse standing on a distant shore far from us. Although in one sense this can seem to be true at certain times, it actually misses the point. We not only look to Jesus externally as the source of light, but we must begin to fully comprehend that His light is *within* us, shining out of us. We actually become that light in the darkness, as the indwelling Spirit shines outward. We need to shift our focus from the external Jesus-lamp to the internal Spirit-lamp, which is reality for born-again believers.

"For you were once darkness, but now you are light in the Lord. Live as children of light (for the fruit of the light consists in all goodness, righteousness and truth) and find out what pleases the Lord. Have nothing to do with the fruitless deeds of darkness, but rather expose them. For it is shameful even to mention what the disobedient do in secret. But everything exposed by the light becomes visible, for it is light that makes everything visible. This is why it is said: 'Wake up, O sleeper, rise from the dead, and Christ will shine on you.'" (Ephesians 5:8-14). We have a daily choice to make; we can either walk in the darkness or we can walk in the light of His presence and power. *"...God is light; in him there is no darkness at all. If we claim to have fellowship with him yet walk in the darkness, we lie and do not live by the truth. But if we walk in the light, as he is in the light, we have fellowship with one another, and the blood of Jesus, his Son, purifies us from all sin."* (1 John 1:5-7). *"He wraps himself in light as a garment"* (Psalm 104:2a). *"His splendor was like the sunrise: rays flashed from his hand, where his power was hidden."* (Habakkuk 3:4). *"...Let the light of your face shine upon us, O Lord."* (Psalm 4:6b).

These passages indicate that Jesus is a radiant source of powerful light. We, too, have a responsibility to flee from sin and to embrace this source of light. Jesus was the great light shining in the darkness of Galilee that had been prophesied in Isaiah chapter nine (see Matthew 4:16; John 8:12). Jesus commanded us to become like Himself and to let our lights shine before other men (Matthew 5:14-16). As we become more like our Savior, we, too, permit the transforming power of this spiritual light to shine out of us. We become a radiant source of hope in the midst of the darkness surrounding us. Hope brings light into the circumstances of life, whereas hopelessness keeps one mired down in depressing darkness.

I am grateful to an elderly woman prophet, Mamie Jo Hunter of Atlanta, Georgia. She taught me an important insight about the power of the eye. Whenever she met with someone she politely requested that they look her directly in the eye. She knew that secrets were revealed while looking into someone's eyes. This was a helpful tool that aided her in discernment, counsel, and prophecy. I have taken this "tool" into the tool chest of my own ministry. I've studied this matter further and have found ample Scriptural support for the eye as the emitter of the condition of the spirit within. A major text is from the Gospel of Matthew, in which Jesus said, *"The eye is the lamp of the body. If your eyes are good, your whole body will be full of light. But if your eyes are bad, your whole body will be full of darkness. If then the light within you is darkness, how great is that darkness!"* (Matthew 6:22-23; emphasis added). Parallel passages on the eye as the lamp are in Luke 8:16-17 and Luke 11:33-36. But, this is not simply a metaphor. There is significant spiritual truth within this concept.

A lamp is an emitter of light, not a receiver. Lamps give off light. They don't suck in darkness. Light is emitted as photons, with two types of physical properties – a wave and a particle, which are sent outward on a mission from their source. To the best of my knowledge of physics, there are no such things as "darktons" or anti-photons that mask or suck up light when you turn off the light switch! Rather, photons are a positive force – an emitted substance with energy that permeates into darkness. Darkness is the absence of photons of light. [As a sidebar comment – Given that God is the source of all spiritual light, there must be deep darkness in hell, because none of God's virtue is wasted on that God-forsaken place. An eternity in that darkness will be an unforgettable eternity.]

Now ponder this for a minute…Jesus said that our eyes are *lamps*. From a heavenly perspective the eyes of a disciple of Jesus are like laser beams emitting the light of the Holy Spirit's indwelling holiness, power, and redemptive purpose! Jesus is saying that what comes out of the eyes is vitally important. But, that's not the way we tend to think of the eye's function. We're typically mindful of what we receive with our eyes, rather than what we declare with our eyes. Brothers and sisters, did you realize that your eyes make declarations! Your eyes are weapons of spiritual warfare.

When a disciple of Jesus looks at someone or something, it produces an effect on the object for the benefit of the Kingdom of God. It is an act of reclamation of the object we're staring upon at that time. Without speaking any words, we are salt and we are light in any setting. Just being there in a place has an effect in the spirit realm! If we were an angelic or demonic being, we could "see" the light emitted from a disciple of Jesus. Furthermore, I speculate that the intensity of that light would be proportional to the holiness and love emitted by the disciple.

To the converse, *"Haughty eyes and a proud heart, the lamp of the wicked, are sin!"* (Proverbs 21:4). The eye is a "lamp" revealing the condition of the heart, either good or bad. For instance, haughtiness and pride are also broadcast out of the eye. David wrote during a time of despair, *"…even the light has gone from my eyes."* (Psalm 38:10). As he was losing hope, his eyes manifested the diminution of light. The eyes reveal the current condition of the heart.

[Jesus used a related analogy concerning the mouth in Matthew 15:10-20. In this parallel teaching, He said it is more important what comes out of the mouth rather than what enters the mouth, such as food. He was referring to speech as that which came out and revealed the condition of the heart, as opposed to food that entered the mouth. In essence, what we say reveals more about the condition of the heart than does what we eat.]

Mamie Jo Hunter and I have both witnessed the principle of *the eye is the lamp of the body* revealing the condition of one's spirit. It is a powerful tool in ministry and in counseling. Often after I have finished preaching at a venue, many people will come forward for prayer or a word of encouragement. Sometimes they stand in long lines for hours just to have a brief time to express their individual concerns. What I have observed hundreds of times is that their eyes seldom conceal what is buried inside. It is difficult for a lying spirit to not reveal some sign(s). Not that I am perfect or have arrived. That is not the case. I am growing and I feel as if I'm still a rookie learning this aspect of prophetic ministry. But, when looking into a person's eyes, some of the secrets of his or her heart are often revealed. His or her eyes are declaring many messages…for instance, shame, or a painful relationship, or a lack of trust, or a lack of receiving nurture as a child from a parent, or fears, or even the desires of the heart. Appropriately spoken prophetic words can then expose in the light those things hidden in darkness (see John 3:19-20). This spiritual gift can discern the heart of total strangers. In some instances I actually prefer to not know anything about the person in advance. By the Holy Spirit's revelation into the situation, tailor-made prophetic words of encouragement, or counsel, or rebuke are offered (see Matthew 10:26-27). And, the eyes play a major part in this revelatory recognition. *"A rich man may be wise in his own eyes, but a poor man who has discernment sees through him."* (Proverbs 28:11). The eyes reveal both light and darkness.

We must be mindful of pursuing a life of righteousness and holiness. King David wrote, *"May integrity and uprightness protect me, because my hope is in you."* (Psalm 25:21). There is a direct relationship between living righteously and the intensity of the light emanating from us. *"The path of the righteous is like the first gleam of dawn, shining ever brighter till the full light of day. But the way of the wicked is like deep darkness; they do not know what makes them stumble."* (Proverbs 4:18-19). *"Arise, shine, for your light has come, and the glory of the Lord rises upon you. See, darkness covers the earth and thick darkness is over the peoples, but the Lord rises upon you and his glory appears over you. Nations will come to your light, and kings to the brightness of your dawn. Lift up your eyes and look about you: All assemble and come to you; your sons come from afar, and your daughters are carried on the arm. Then you will look and be radiant, your heart will throb and swell with joy..."* (Isaiah 60:1-5). Many believers consider this passage to refer to the final days or the Millennium. I believe there is a "now" manifestation and reward for those who choose to walk in righteousness and holiness that empowers a disciple even while on the earth. *"Those who are wise will shine like the brightness of the heavens, and those who lead many to righteousness, like the stars for ever and ever."* (Daniel 12:3). And, referring to the end of the age Jesus said, *"Then the righteous will shine like the sun in the kingdom of their Father. He who has ears, let him hear."* (Matthew 13:43).

Friends, we have a responsibility to grow up and permit the light of Jesus to shine out of us with ever-increasing brightness. Let your light shine before men. Become the generator of light in your world. When this occurs, we will be photons of hope, not "darktons" of hopelessness!

—

2

THE EVIL GRIP OF HOPELESSNESS

"Didn't I tell you, 'Don't raise my hopes'?"

~ 2 Kings 4:28b

The Shunammite woman shared this distressing verse with the prophet Elisha in a moment of desperation. Her only son, who was the result of a prior fulfilled prophecy, had just died. And with him, so did her hope. Her plea to Elisha was rational and it was from her crushed heart. Years before this incident she had been shocked at his prophecy that she and the elderly father would bear a son. Back then she declared in dismay, *"No, my lord…Don't mislead your servant, O man of God!"* (2 Kings 4:16b). Now the promised child had just died. And with his death, she had fallen under the evil grip of hopelessness. But, by the power of the Almighty, Elisha restored the boy back to life.

In a prior similar hopeless situation, the prophet Elijah (Elisha's mentor) was directed to visit a widow mother in Zarephath (see 1 Kings 17:7-24). She and her only son were destitute, and all she had was enough flour to bake one final cake for a final meal, before she and her son would die of starvation. Elijah was filled with faith and essentially told her ~ *"Bake me a cake as fast as you can; Roll it; Roll it; And mark it with a T; And, throw it in the oven for…me"*. His request was irrational and inconsiderate in the natural realm. But, it was a divine test of her character and her faith. She received the reward for acting appropriately, and later in the story the prophet restored the life to her son.

The two mothers of Shunem and Zarephath had fallen into hopelessness. Their situations appeared beyond any reasonable measure of hope. To almost everyone facing the cold hard fact of a dead loved one, the prospect of resurrection seems extremely remote, if not impossible. But, God showed up at each of the two ladies' parties, and their sons became living testimonies of God's intervention.

Hope is the bedrock upon which faith is established. If hope is the bedrock, then faith is the structure built upon it. You can't build a durable faith-house without a good foundation of hope. One cannot demonstrate faith without a measure of hope. In my book, <u>Praying Faith</u>, the meaning of faith was defined as *risk-taking belief in action*. So, although linked, faith and hope are not the same thing. It is impossible to have faith without hope. But, you can have a measure of hope without exercising faith. Faith builds upon hope. Thus, hope is the platform or the foundation.

THE IMPOSSIBLE, POSSIBLE, PROBABLE, AND PROPHETIC

On the path toward genuine faith there are four "levels" from hopelessness to hope that we can choose to adopt. The first of the four stages is the *Impossible*, the second is the *Possible*, the third is the *Probable*, and fourth is the *Prophetic*. One may have a mental or spiritual outlook at any one of the four stages concerning a particular issue they are facing. For instance, when confronted with a bad report from the physician about a debilitating disease, the individual will believe the medical report to a varying degree and adopt one of the four perspectives. She or he can believe the "bad" report and lose all hope. Or, she or he can come to a different conclusion.

It takes no risk to adopt the first condition of the *impossible*. That option comes easily and naturally to many of us as we analyze the severity of the physician's report. It takes no hope to accept this depressing news. Hope actually is the initial ingredient in the remedy to ascend out of the *impossible* to a higher level. Without hope, one will remain in the pit of despair and will not seek out creative paths to get out of those negative circumstances.

To go beyond the realm of the *impossible*, we need to demonstrate a higher level of optimism. It takes hope to ascend to the second stage of the *possible*, as well to continue on to the subsequent third and fourth levels. Without hope one will always remain in the pessimistic camp of the *impossible*. As hope is mustered, the ability to assume risk in our actions is elevated sequentially at each subsequent level. Scripture tells us that nothing is impossible for our omnipotent Almighty Creator, unless of course His written Word has explicitly precluded it. Transitioning our outlook from the *impossible* to the *possible* certainly is an accomplishment. However, in many regards this transition falls far short of stimulating any change that will result in the desired outcome. But, it is still an essential step. You can't begin to walk in genuine faith, until you first accept that with God all things are possible.

If one does not believe that it is even remotely *possible* to heal the sick or cast out demons, then she or he will never attempt any actions that would result in the sick being healed or the demonically influenced from being set free. The same is true for praying that someone would be raised from the dead. Our theological beliefs can impair our ability to have hope and thus faith. If it is considered to be *impossible* due to one's theology, then you might as well throw the baby out with the bath water, because it just isn't going to happen.

Cessationism is a theological teaching that doubts and restricts the power of the Holy Spirit to operate today. Those who follow this teaching do not expect miracles to happen today, or if so only on rare occasions. In addition, Cessationists tend to re-interpret the meaning of the term "miracle" to diminish it to something that is remarkable or grand, yet certainly doable without the power of the Holy Spirit. They might use the term "miracle", but they mean something far less than that. The term has been neutered.

According to Psalm 18:25-29, God only reveals to us what we desire to see of His attributes, character, and power. We limit what He wants to show us. Therefore, if our theology has already influenced us to not expect the miraculous, then that's precisely what God will reveal to us. Our attitude toward His power will limit His power to move in our circumstances. Those who expect miracles to be routine in life will find that miracles happen far more often than those who doubt it.

Unfortunately Cessationism is common among many Evangelical

and Protestant denominations. It is my prayer that the Almighty will be merciful and reveal Himself as a miracle worker, in spite of the stiff-necked resistance of those who advocate Cessationism. All it takes is one good "power encounter" by the Holy Spirit and then a lifetime of aberrant theology can be turned on its head. One good miracle or a vision or a prescient dream or a word of knowledge can counteract years of erroneous theology that denies the reality that the Holy Spirit is alive and well and working in the miraculous routinely.

There is a simple phrase often quoted in some circles worth considering, *"What you believe you receive."* Many motivational speakers say this or similar things. I often hear this motivational expression within the African-American community. It is somewhat true. I don't entirely agree with it, but it serves a valid point worthy of consideration. If you don't believe in something, you're unlikely to pursue it. And, without pursuit you won't obtain the desired goal.

Recall the words of Thomas, when he said in dismay to the other apostles concerning their claims that Jesus had been raised back to life from the dead, *"Unless I see the nail marks in his hands and put my finger where the nails were, and put my hand into his side, I will not believe it."* (John 20:25b). Thomas was honest and had no faith, because his reservoir of hope had been depleted. He knew a lot of facts about the crucifixion that contradicted the possibility of Jesus being raised from the dead. He was despondent and had abandoned hope, including even that it was *possible* for Jesus to be alive. Mere words from his colleagues were not enough to break through his spirit of disbelief. Recollection of Jesus' own prior words didn't have any effect upon Thomas. To him at that juncture, Jesus was still dead. I admire Thomas' honesty, but his disbelief was less than admirable. Understandable, but not admirable. An analytical mind can be a great hindrance to faith.

Doubting Thomas represents many of us when we face adverse circumstances. Circumstances are the fire extinguishers of faith. We cry out, *"I'll believe it when I see it."* But, that is not faith. Once you see it, it is established as fact. That which is seen or known requires no faith. Not one ounce! Faith only operates while the object of desire is still unseen (see Hebrews 11:1-6). Once you actually see something you had desired, it doesn't take any faith. Too late, the time for faith is over. The time for sight has begun. Faith and sight don't belong in the same sentence. They are oxymorons. Faith is a challenge; sight is easy and natural. So, *"I'll believe it when I see it"* is not true. Re-orient your thinking. We should quit saying that phrase, since we are really saying, *"I'll know it when I see it."*

We begin to see results once we believe in the *probable*! Jesus had an interaction with a desperate man who was requesting help with his son, who was influenced by a demon. When asked whether he believed Jesus could do what he desired, the man replied, *"I believe; help me overcome my unbelief."* (Mark 9:24). He was demonstrating a *probable* level of understanding and commitment. Jesus was gracious to him for the honest, limited, yet real level of confidence he demonstrated. For many of us, it can be a giant stretch to go from *possible* to *probable* in mental assent. When our words declare that it is *likely* that something will happen when we pray or take action in spite of the apparent circumstances, we're making progress on the road toward faith. After all, you only need faith the size of a mustard seed.

However, the ultimate standard of faith is 100% risk-taking belief in action. I term this level as *prophetic*, as it is the personal confidence that God will certainly do what He has revealed. It lacks doubt. It is a *"Lord, I'm getting out of the boat to walk on water"* time. I am privileged to know many prophetic individuals, who routinely receive rhema revelation from the Holy Spirit. I would consider a small subset of them as being modern prophets. The revelations they receive provide confidence about God's intended course of action in a particular situation, provided the recipients interpret and apply the rhema revelations correctly. In Praying Faith some examples were included demonstrating how God's revealed rhema intentions were fulfilled in agreement with the advance notices received prophetically.

Faith at this level of hope is indeed *prophetic*. It is enabled with our Holy Spirit's power to see that the "word" takes effect. This *exusia* type of declared *prophetic* reality can establish God's intentions on earth. Just as Jesus, the Word, became flesh and dwelt among us, so the rhema word becomes reality and dwells among us. But, believing and acting in the *prophetic* takes a heightened level of risk-taking belief in action! It takes assurance and confidence.

In this book we'll consider examples of elevating one's mind and spirit out of the pit of the *impossible* into the progressively higher realms of the *possible*, the *probable*, and the *prophetic*. Some of the examples involved declarations of God's intentions via a prophetic individual. It is a goal of this book to demonstrate by examples what Jesus Christ is capable of doing through a yielded servant. He loves us and desires for our best outcome. He desires for us to have hope and to give hope away to others.

As one who is increasingly being stretched by rhema revelation and prophetic ministry, I have observed that faith, confidence, and prophecy are intertwined like a triple-stranded cord. They are inseparable attributes of one another. Sometimes an individual will ask, *"Was that 'word' a prophecy or a statement of faith?"* I honestly have a hard time answering that question, as these two things seem to flow together. It isn't an either/or situation, rather it is a fusion where the boundaries are hard to distinguish. If it is true, it's true…doesn't matter what you call it. It is still true. Wouldn't it be wonderful if prophetic men and women were so precise and accurate with a measure of humilty, so that they would cease from using the phrase *"The Lord says"* as a preamble? Why the qualifier? What a prophetic voice says is either true or it isn't. Over time the word will be judged as either true or false. The opening preface *"The Lord says"* should be largely irrelevant, unless the person is insecure and just wants attention.

Let us strive toward living in the *prophetic*, that which involves the certainties of life. Let us be quick to move from the *impossible* to the *possible* to the *probable* to the *prophetic,* as we face the walls of resistance and difficulties. At whatever level you are currently operating in, step up, take your place, and then you'll be moved to an even higher level of hope.

A PROPHETIC WORD
WAS A KEY TO DELIVERANCE

As an example of how the gift of prophecy can impact the hope within an individual, let me share the following story. Once while preaching at Grace Covenant Church near Chicago, Illinois I was prompted by the Holy Spirit to stop in the middle of the message for a diversion. I mentioned several significant dreams from ~ 1987, when I was living in London. One dream was about going down into hell, and the other was about a demon-possessed dog. Then, I declared that I believed that the

Holy Spirit is concerned by the profit motive of some *for-profit Christian counseling centers*. This concern is not that service is being provided, rather that in some cases the counselors profit financially while *not* setting the captives free from their afflictions.

One role of the *real* Church Universal is to help shepherd and counsel believers of Jesus. I also believe it should be free-of-charge and untainted by profit motives. We are to pray and counsel the afflicted through their areas of weakness and pain and to help them understand the consequences of their choices. If the Church was working well as intended by God, there should be a reduced need for man-made for-profit Christian counseling centers. In some cases those businesses can make individuals in spiritual and emotional need become dependent upon their counseling services. Fee-for-service counseling sessions can create a dependent environment that fails to meet Biblical principles for mental and spiritual well-being. If the Church was doing what it was supposed to be doing, we could limit the drain of financial resources from those in pain. So, there are problems on both sides – the Church isn't doing enough, and in some cases, Christian counseling centers are doing too much (i.e., profiting with questionable motives).

At the conclusion of preaching in Chicago, a woman named Tammy approached me to ask, *"Your comments about for-profit Christian counseling centers were quite strong. Isn't there some value in this type of service?"* Having discerned something from her comments, I was prompted to reply, *"If the Spirit is cautioning you about for-profit Christian counseling centers, shouldn't you check this out further using the Bible?"* As these words were shared, she appeared to be physically and emotionally shaken. The Holy Spirit was working through the words I had spoken regarding the two former dreams and regarding counseling for profit. I further clarified these challenging words, *"The Bible instructs that the path to recovery includes acknowledgement of sin, repentance, forgiveness, reconciliation, and restoration, and in certain cases deliverance. Once the cycle is completed, the 'captives' are set free! They are no longer in bondage. They aren't paying someone a fee in perpetuity to be 'maintained'. They are free. There is nothing explicit in the Bible in support of the institution of for-profit Christian counseling centers or of being paid to counsel someone in need. Therefore, please re-read your Bible with this perspective in mind, and ask the Spirit for revelation."* This brought to her deep conviction, even though I didn't know anything about this woman's past or present condition.

I felt that she needed to hear this "hard" blunt word. Sometimes, you must speak directly to produce the desired affect. Some of us are hard nuts to crack! In these cases a rebuke cloaked in sentimentality would not hit the mark. Many "fathers" are better equipped than "mothers" to bring this type of corrective word or disciplinary word. Oh God, please raise up more "fathers" of the faith! I believe we have drifted too much toward a "feminized" standard of ministry. It is out of balance.

Later when I left the gathering I asked the pastor, Derek Kuhn, about this woman. He replied that she had been dependent on for-profit Christian counseling sessions for at least two years concerning the pains of her past. He speculated that it cost hundreds of dollars each month to maintain Tammy's psychological "treatments" for many years. He and I both remarked that the Holy Spirit had touched her deeply, and it was our prayer/declaration of agreement that she would be genuinely "delivered" that Sunday from that which was shackling her to the past. Ironically, the very thing she believed would help set her free was actually another device that was keeping her enslaved to the memories of the past.

She wrote to me later saying that, effective that Sunday, she made a decision to change (including leaving her dependency on for-profit counseling). She was on the path toward recovery and was eventually set free to more fully recognize God's "A-plan" for her life. Jesus provided a precious victory that day in her life, and it didn't cost her a penny! It is worth noting that the night prior to our meeting in Chicago, Tammy had two dreams. One was about "going down into hell" and the other was about a "demon-possessed dog", thus resembling the two dreams I had shared as a preamble to the challenging word about profiting from counseling.

Jesus echoed the words of Isaiah 61 when he declared that He came to set the captives free! He didn't come to merely 'maintain' them. He came to free us from sin and its consequences. Sometimes God will send a minister or other person to bring correction or rebuke to open our eyes to a new reality. I thank God for those who speak "truth in love" and don't merely give the sugar coated fuzzy-white-lamb Jesus stuff. Sure, Jesus is partly revealed by that image, but that is far from disclosing the breadth of His attributes. We need the truth, the whole truth, and nothing but the truth, so help us God. Anything less will harm us. *"Then you will know the truth and the truth shall set you free."* (John 8:32).

Please note that I do recognize that some mental health professionals are well trained and effective as physicians or counselors, who can be very helpful in treating certain psychological problems. I'm not criticizing these professionals, as some mental health issues are serious enough to warrant intervention by a psychiatrist or a counselor, and in some cases including the use of therapeutic medicines. Examples can include neurological injury from trauma, genetic syndromes with mental impairment, schizophrenia, depression, bipolar disorder, obsessive-compulsive disorder, and dementia. These conditions can cause a profound disillusionment and hopelessness.

However, these mental health professionals must strive to genuinely set the captives free and not simply maintain a roster of patients in perpetuity for the sake of assured income as a physician or counselor. In addition, these professionals should not seek to replace the role of ministers and other spiritual counselors, who will often perform counseling (and in some cases deliverance ministry) at no cost. Furthermore, it is incumbent on those believers within the Kingdom of God with relevant spiritual gifts and callings to step up. They need to volunteer to help those afflicted with mental or psychosocial problems.

At present it is very difficult to locate Bible-based believers who are psychiatrists (board certified MDs specializing in mental health) and to a lesser extent psychologists. This is due to the fact that psychiatrists, who are coincidentally genuine believers, are rare. My family has the privilege of working with a delightful Christian psychiatrist, who has aided our family with a mental health issue. He has demonstrated compassionate care with awareness of the dynamic of humans having three components – a physical body, a soul (mind and emotions), and an eternal spirit. It is typical for the vast majority of psychiatrists to deny or disregard the "spirit" component. They embrace the secular principle of *dualism*, expounded by the philosopher Descartes.

Let us pray that God will raise up more believers as Judeo-Christian psychiatrists (and psychologists), who will bring relief to the afflicted within the context of a Biblical worldview and a keen awareness of spiritual warfare. An affected individual might need only prayer and counseling, another might need deliverance ministry, and yet another might need the diagnosis and aid of a psychiatrist. Oh, may the Kingdom of God invade and transform the mental health industry from the inside out, so that the whole being of the afflicted – mental, physical, and spiritual – is addressed by the healing touch of the Lord. May He send His mercy and healing down. May He raise up those skilled in bringing healing, deliverance, and hope. May He set the captives free!

THE OCTOPUS OF HOPELESSNESS

The spirit of hopelessness has many tentacles, each with multiple suction cups or points of adhesion, like those of a giant octopus. While scuba diving in Hawaii I captured a medium sized eight-legged specimen. I placed it upon my buoyancy compensator on my chest that keeps a diver neutrally buoyant. The creature rapidly wrapped all of its tentacles around my torso, and the suction cups were activated. We posed for an underwater photograph of an octopus wrapped around my chest. Then, it became time to remove it, but it was quite an effort to pry it off. I could get some of the suction cups free to loosen a tentacle, but then when my hands moved on to the other tentacles, the free tentacles would easily reattach. It was an interesting dilemma. There are so many points of contact, it is difficult to free oneself, even from a small octopus.

The suction cups on the tentacles of hopelessness put a stranglehold on each suffering woman or man. The multiple manifestations of hopelessness drain the life force out of someone. The synergistic suction of many cups, each representing a point of pain (e.g., loneliness, depression, or disappointment) makes escape difficult for the victim. Once caught, it is hard to remove its tentacles. Once the octopus hits and settles in, it is in for the long haul. Isn't hopelessness just like this? One interesting observation made by a master diver was that if you place your hand on the "head" of the octopus, you can stimulate the animal's nervous system to relax and loosen its grip. By analogy we should attack the "head", not merely the multitude of symptoms of hopelessness.

Hopelessness has a myriad number of manifestations. To illuminate many of the suction cups on the tentacles of this octopus of the spirit of hopelessness, I have created a list of "tendencies" that I consider to be associated with either hope or hopelessness (see Table I below). This is not intended as a scientific research summary, rather just as a list of characteristics or attributes that likely underscore hope vs. hopelessness. A person afflicted by the mental and spiritual pain of hopelessness will demonstrate many of these characteristics or tendencies. The afflicted will have a difficult time being set free, due to the multiple points of contact. Attempting to remedy the problem by working at it piecemeal one item at a time doesn't address the fullness of the condition. If you address only one of the attitudes or attributes, there are still many other suction cups on various tentacles firmly attached.

TABLE I

HOPE	HOPELESSNESS
goals	no goals
focused on a favorable future	focused on the immediate problem
significance	mediocrity
appreciate life	apathetic
optimism	pessimism
builds faith with expectations	produces skepticism with doubts
altruism	self-centered
giving	receiving
hard working	striving for existence
productive	inactive or merely busy
freedom	enslavement
joy & laughter	sadness & anger
offer a hand out	expect a hand out
overcomer	victim
appropriate risk-taking	dangerous risk-taking
cherish life	suicidal
wholeness	brokenness
life-giving	draining
build up others	tear down others
health	illness
financial sufficiency & content	financial dependence & poverty
know your purpose	see no purpose

HOPE	HOPELESSNESS
advance the Kingdom of God	survive in a holding pattern
patient	impatient
eternal perspective	temporal focus
solve the problem	are the problem
content with met "needs"	desiring "wants"
balanced mind	imbalanced mind
sound reasoning	delusions
fulfilled	frustrated & empty
recipient of blessings	recipient of curses
angelic assistance	demonic harrassment
obedient to God	disobedient to God
enthusiasm	depression & psychoses
believe God's promises	skeptical of God's existence or character
trust authority	distrust authority
humorous	burdensome
"parent" to others	demanding "child"
see "light"	see "darkness"
see "potential"	see "nothing good"
firm foundation for faith	unstable foundation
repent for sin	remorse about sin
give forgiveness	harbor unforgiveness
victorious	defeated
positive influence	negative influence
attract most people	attract only malcontents
motivated	lazy
gratitude	bitterness
trust in God and reliable people	do not trust in God or people
persevere in trials	despair in trials
pleased with own self	displeased with own self
humble	proud
social	lonely
smiles	tears

HOPE	HOPELESSNESS
take the responsibility for error	blame others for error
attain accomplishments	shame over failures
receive honor	receive judgement
priorities in balance	priorities out of balance
elevate the "important"	elevate the "trivial"
make history	read about it
look to the future with anticipation	return to your past
easily make friends	alienate others
dreamer	blocked creativity
bless others	curse others
sow expecting a harvest	wish to win a lottery
generous	hoarding
nourish others	drain others
see the solution	see the problem

From some limited experiences in deliverance ministry, it becomes apparent that demonic forces enable the spirit of hopelessness. There are often spiritual forces behind the mental issues of hopelessness. When an entire gang of demons attack *en masse*, one can end up with a *Legion* of demonic voices affecting an individual. In aggregate each of these properties or characteristics gangs up on the mind and physical body of the affected person, further creating a deepened sense of hopelessness. Jesus said that unless the house is swept clean and replaced with good things, the entourage will return and the latter state will be worse than the former.

Now is the time for a call to action to confront the *Spirit of Hopelessness*. I anticipate some dark days are on the horizon in which this "force" will have an increasingly grim role to play in the minds of individuals, societies, and nations. Furthermore, I predict that there will be a specific *sign* from God when this happens. Many people, who currently consider themselves to be "religious" Christians or Jews, will come to us and plead, *"My prayers are not answered, but your prayers are! Will you pray for me, because*

God listens to your requests?" That will be the *sign*.

There are many religious people living in the Western World today who are living under the *illusion of blessing*. Prayers of the faithful and obedient will always be answered, but the prayers of the posers and pretenders will not. Some of the illusion of blessing is conveniently due to living in the affluence of the West. The "apparent" blessings have little to do with their individual walk of faith or relationship with the Almighty. It is more "coincidental" blessing by association with an affluent society. Many attending multi-million dollar megachurches or cathedrals will soon wake up to a new reality. They had been living in an *illusion of blessing*.

When the security rug is pulled out from underneath them, many will scatter and lose what little sense of faith that they thought they had. But, these foolish individuals (and there will be many of them) had not purchased oil for their lamps when it was readily available in the market. There will be division and separation between the "real" and the "pretenders", between the wheat and the tares, between the so-called Christians and the genuine disciples of Jesus. I firmly believe these days are fast approaching. Days of great shaking are coming…and especially with great consequences for those living in the comfortable Western World.

So, in that day, be mindful to keep your relationship with the Lord Jesus strong. Remain obedient and strive to live in righteousness. There are many promises in the Scriptures that are dependent upon you living in righteousness. They are conditional promises. You can't claim a Scriptural promise if you are walking in disobedience to His principles.

SORRY I MISSED THE PARTY, BUT I WAS DEAD!

Let's consider one of the most hopeless situations fathomable. In 1914 Sir Ernest Shackleton led a team of men on an adventure expedition to Antarctica onboard the ship, *Endurance*. Their goal was to make an overland crossing of the frigid no-man's land. They planned to navigate by sea and land some of the most treacherous forsaken territory on earth. However, their sailing vessel became lodged in a solid ice pack early in the venture. They had not expected or necessarily planned for this particular hazard. It must have been a tremendous surprising setback. The crew was forced to abandon the ship during the fall of 1915, which was relatively early in their intended journey. The ice ruptured the ship's hull under intense pressure. Thus, staying there on the solid ice pack of the Weddell Sea was not a viable option. So, the crew of the *Endurance* had to adapt during this life-threatening crisis.

Shackleton and his crew were forced to improvise a survival strategy prior to the advent of radio communication to request a rescue team. They gathered from the ship their essential cold-weather clothing, food rations, and other gear. They set out by foot pulling along small boats containing their gear over the pack ice. It was extremely difficult and perilous. Quoting from the biography about Shackleton's journey:

> *His face was grave. He explained it was imperative that all weight be reduce to the barest minimum…Speaking with the utmost conviction, Shackleton pointed out that no article was of any value when weighed against their ultimate survival, and he exhorted them to be ruthless in ridding themselves of every unnecessary ounce, regardless of value. After he had spoken, he reached under his parka and took out a gold cigarette case and several gold sovereigns [i.e., British money] and threw them into the snow at his feet. Then he opened the Bible Queen Alexandra had given them and ripped out the flyleaf and the page containing the Twenty-third Psalm. He also tore out the page of the book of Job with this verse on it: 'Out of whose womb came the ice? And the hoary frost of Heaven, who hath gendered it? The waters are hid as with a stone. And the face of the deep is frozen.' And he laid the Bible in the snow and walked away.* (Endurance, Alfred Lansing, p. 57).

Their phenomenal struggle for survival by land and sea in extremely dangerous conditions was made possible by the tangible hope projected by their calm courageous leader. For a total of 17 months they were essentially in suspended animation, surviving one day at a time. They endured extreme frigid conditions and countless obstacles at sea and on land that would have discouraged the most hardened sailor or fisherman. To the commander's credit, his biography records:

> *This indomitable self-confidence of Shackleton's took the form of optimism. And it worked in two ways: It set men's souls on fire; … just to be in his presence was an experience. It was what made Shackleton so great a leader.* (Endurance, Alfred Lansing, p. 90).

Finally, a small expeditionary unit led by Shackleton separated from the rest and crossed over a glacial landmass. The small band appeared at an inhabited fishing camp to the disbelief of those present, as well as to those around the world, who later heard the report. Shackleton appeared out of nowhere as if "resurrected" from a presumed dead condition. If I were him, I would have been tempted to jokingly greet the wide-eyed witnesses with, *"Sorry I missed the party, but I was dead!"*

While in the midst of extreme hardships, their team stayed focused on a positive outcome even though it seemed futile that it could be remotely possible. By focusing with hope on all of the variables within their control (e.g., food, shelter, clothing, persistence, and hard work), they surprised the world with their resourcefulness and resilience. I doubt that many of us "softies" today could have performed half as well under that level of near hopelessness. Yet, not one life was lost during this mission!

Shackleton prevailed where many other leaders would have failed. He survived because he never succumbed to the grips of fear, so that his hope remained visibly strong before his crew. A leader must demonstrate hope if he or she desires to influence followers. Napoleon Bonaparte astutely declared, *"A leader is a dealer in hope."* Infectious optimism in Shackleton's case saved lives in the Antarctic. He never permitted the *spirit of hopelessness* to destroy the team's desire for a rescue. By clinging to hope he became like a modern day Lazarus, who denied the grave its sting.

3

A LEAP OF FAITH

I will not die but live, and will proclaim what the Lord has done.

~ Ps. 118:17

Many children have pondered jumping off the roof or a tree with a parachute or a special power-laden suit as Superman. In 1981 and only weeks prior to my marriage I jumped out of a perfectly fine airplane near Lawrence, Kansas at several thousand feet. This jump was recorded as part of a research study on induced stress in the journal, *Science*.

Apparently the apple doesn't fall far from the tree. Reaching further back in time, in the late 1930's my father, his two older brothers Bill and Joe, and cousin Rich fancied themselves parachutists as well. The famous aviatrix, Amelia Earhart, grew up as a child in a home overlooking the Missouri River in Atchison, not far from our family farm. And, sightings of airplanes were drawing looks of fascination throughout the land in that era between World Wars I and II.

Led by the eldest brother, Bill Dooley, the foursome gathered a bed-spread and some baling twine for use as a makeshift parachute. Then, Bill ascended to the top of the steel frame of the windmill used to pump well water on my grandparent's farm. Bill intended to jump with the four corners of the blanket tied by baling twine to his hands. He expected an exhilarating, gentle, yet brief ride to *terra firma*.

But wisdom got the best of his brother Joe, who urged that they should first conduct an experiment with a heavy rock to prove the effectiveness of their strategy. This modified plan spared Uncle Bill a lot of pain and perhaps a few broken bones. The tethered rock sped to the ground lickedy-split. The rock traveled so fast that it hit the horse tank and ruptured the metal bottom of it. Needless to say, this pre-jump experiment got their attention, and diverted an almost certain casualty for one of the Dooley boys.

Oh...I wish my daughter, Catherine, had seen a film of that event from the late 1930's!

What would you do in the following situation? Upon exiting a plane that had not slowed down sufficiently once it reached the relative low altitude of 5,000 feet, the force of the wind of the plane's propeller and momentum blow you straight back into the tail. Both bones in your right forearm are snapped in a moment by contact with the leading surface of the tail's metal edge. You know instantly that you have just lost the use of the right arm that is needed to pull the cord to deploy your parachute. You are dropping in free fall at 130 mph with a right arm resembling the limb of a Raggedy Ann doll, more like gelatin than a solid arm. You now have less than one minute to recover before you would be assured that you would die upon impact. And, you have been trained to know that most severe injuries and fatalities happen upon landing, rather than upon departing the plane. What would you do in this crisis?

This is not a hypothetical scenario. This precise situation literally happened to my precious 20-year old daughter, Catherine, on September 17, 2005 at the Pell City, Alabama airport. One hour away from the airport I received a parent's dreaded nightmare phone call. A man said, *"Mr. Dooley, I'm an emergency medical technician. Your daughter has just injured herself in a sky diving accident. She has a broken arm and possibly other damage. We need to transport her soon to a hospital."* I then spoke with Catherine briefly by phone, before they left in the ambulance for the small regional hospital.

Returning to the freefall, not only did she have a serious arm injury, but she also endured two additional life-threatening problems after hitting the tail section. She crushed her left heel bone upon landing at high speed. And, later that evening the hospital staff in Pell City administered excessive levels of opiate pain killers resulting in respiratory arrest while in the emergency room. What an evening!

When Catherine realized that her arm bones had been snapped, she immediately praised the Creator saying, *"I thank You God that I'm still alive. I know I have a destiny. I will live and I will not die today!"* She was drawing upon Psalm 118:17 (above) and was also mindful of the prophetic "call" upon her life that had not yet been fulfilled. She then managed to reach behind her back while in freefall with her left arm to locate the pull cord for the main chute located on the opposite side of her body. She deployed the main chute and began a gentle glide toward *terra firma*. Then, she sang, *"Holy, Holy, Holy is the Lord God Almighty"* and portions of some other worship songs. Because of her trust in the unseen Creator God and her awareness in part of His plans for her future, she was confident to not despair. She projected hope into the situation.

The devil is a liar. He comes only to steal, kill, and destroy. He wants us to never see into the unseen spiritual realm of the heavenlies, unless that is to only frighten us. He wants us so earthly focused that we're of no heavenly good. The devil wants us consumed by worldly issues. He uses difficult circumstances as the fire extinguishers of faith. But God desires for us to have faith without doubting that He is in control and will see us through. Catherine's hope and faith remained strong in spite of the severe forearm injury and in view of the peril facing her on the ground below.

While landing a parachutist needs both arms to pull down on the two toggles to steer and to brake the forward momentum. With only one arm available, Catherine could only steer a little, and she could not stop her momentum in the final seconds. She knew she would hit the ground at high velocity. This caused her to crush her left heel bone. Not only does Catherine know some of her prophetic destiny in life, but the devil desired to kill her in view of God's favor and calling on her life. The devil tried to kill her the first time in the air and failed. So, he tried a second time on the ground and failed. Then, he tried a third time while in the hospital while she was supposed to be receiving treatments to "stabilize" her condition (an ironic term isn't it?).

But, this third time while in the emergency room I stood over her gray breathless body (albeit she may have had a residual weak pulse). I intervened on her behalf and declared loudly in prayer in the emergency room, *"Catherine, you will live and you will not die today! Jesus has all authority in heaven and on earth. As your father I have the authority over you given in Jesus' name. I declare you will breathe and you will live!"* I continued this until medical intervention, which included Narcan antidote to overcome the huge over-dose of opiates in her body that she should not have been given. My wife, Laura, and our youngest son, Thomas were also there at the foot of the bed praying and watching as the medical staff was mobilized into action as I declared prayer loudly in the emergency room. We also read scrip-tures that night, and one in particular kept resonating in my spirit, *"The name of the Lord is a strong tower; the righteous run to it and are safe."* (Proverbs 18:20). The third episode of the day is reminiscent of the peculiar witty saying, *"A man was taken to the hospital and was seriously injured. Therefore, he shouldn't have gone to the hospital."*

During the first two attempts on her life Catherine had the hope and faith to believe beyond her circumstances. She knew in Whom she had believed and was persuaded that He was able to keep that which had been committed to Him on her behalf. Then, during the third case faith rose up within me to believe beyond her circumstances. Laura and Thomas were there when she was gray and apparently lifeless for multiple minutes. We saw breath come back into her lifeless body. Faith reaches beyond the "reality" of the moment.

To our family and friends in the hospital it was akin to when the *Fourth Man* entered into the fiery furnace with Daniel's three close friends. Oh, everything is different when the *Fourth Man* arrives! May you cry out in your day of great need and see that the arm of the Lord is not too short that He can't reach down and save. May He send the *Fourth Man* to the rescue when you're in the fiery furnace. *"No one whose hope is in you [God] will ever be put to shame…"* (Psalm 25:3a).

Catherine subsequently endured pain-filled recoveries from surgeries on her arm and heel. But, we are so proud of Catherine for her hope-based faith in Jesus that literally saw her through multiple life-threatening crises on one evening. She now has a remarkable testimony of faith test-ed by fire that few believers can match. Few, if any, can declare that they were struck by a flying airplane and lived to tell the story! Few can declare that they survived three separate life-threatening "accidents" in a single day! To God Almighty, El Shaddai, be all the glory.

As the Scripture says in Psalm 118:7, *"I will not die but live, and will pro-claim what the Lord has done."* I don't know about you, but it is doubtful that many of us would respond as well as Catherine. Many of us would have panicked and likely suffered a worse fate. Her trust in God had already been well distilled prior to this crisis (see Proverbs 3:5-7). She already knew God's character and reliability, before she encountered the storm. Catherine knew that she had an *Anchor* that would hold in spite of the storm, just like the song **"The Anchor Holds"** by Lawrence Chewning and Ray Boltz:

> *I have journeyed, Through the long, dark night*
> *Out on the open sea*
> *By faith alone, Sight unknown*
> *And yet His eyes were watching me*

> *(CHORUS) The anchor holds, Though the ship is battered*
> *The anchor holds, Though the sails are torn*
> *I have fallen on my knees, As I faced the raging seas*
> *The anchor holds, In spite of the storm*

> *I've had visions, I've had dreams*
> *I've even held them in my hand*
> *But I never knew, They would slip right through*
> *Like they were only grains of sand*

> *I have been young, But I am older now*
> *And there has been beauty, That these eyes have seen*
> *But it was in the night, Through the storms of my life*
> *Oh, that's where God proved, His love to me*

My friend Dr. Liu mentioned to me that the state seal and flag of Rhode Island features an anchor and the word "Hope". The pioneering spirit of the original colonists in New England required a lot of hope to endure the hardships of the Trans-Atlantic journeys. Upon arrival they needed to establish a foothold in a foreign land without the conveniences of their former homeland. Many of the original colonists were devout disciples of Jesus. Many were known as "Dissenters", risk-taking non-conformists who were not satisfied with religion-as-usual. They were the objects of scorn and persecution on behalf of the established Church of

England that had unfortunately diverged away from the pure root of the Gospel into the land of milk-toast religion. Some of the radical Dissenters were Quakers, others were Methodist followers of the Wesley brothers, others were Baptists, others were descendents of the Scottish Presbyterian Reformers, and many were captivated by the messages of the trail-riding evangelist George Whitefield (albeit some of them were born after the founding of Rhode Island).

To these pioneering disciples in Rhode Island and all of New England, the anchor's meaning was obvious. The Rhode Island General Assembly first adopted the Seal in 1664. It is likely that the symbolism and word "Hope" was inspired by Hebrews 6:18-19, *"...we who have fled to take hold of the hope offered to us may be greatly encouraged. We have this hope as an anchor for the soul, firm and secure..."* (Illustrations of the Seals, Arms and Flags of Rhode Island, Howard M. Chapin, Rhode Island Historical Society, 1930). To the founders of Rhode Island, their hope was in the reliability of God Almighty to perform that which He had declared. He was dependable when nothing else was assured and much was at risk.

THE FREEDOM OF FLIGHT

Flying is a symbol of freedom and power to overcome one's circumstances. It is a metaphor for the impossible, unless you're already a bird. I have had countless dreams in which I fly like a bird or Superman. In one dream while working on a farm I walked into a botanical gardens of the nearby village, then arrived at a ministry gathering inside of a building. Several dozen folks were sitting in a circle, and it was hospitable and friendly. I was very much "at home" there in this informal ministry gathering. One-by-one each presented what they had...a song, a Scripture reading, a piece of art, or whatever. Each one rose to the center of the room for his or her portion. There was honor given to each person, regardless of his or her level of maturity or presentation. First Nations Peoples (e.g., Native Americans) refer to this as a "Talking Circle". Everyone faces one another and as protocol dictates each may contribute something on a level playing field. This type of fellowship gathering enhances interpersonal relationships. It encourages and bolsters the spiritual gifts within each individual. Western churches should strive to foster this pattern in their own gatherings.

In this dream, two women approached me gleefully with expectation and whispered that I had something *"powerful and prophetic"* for them. I waited for my turn in the rotation of the circle. Then, I levitated up out of my seat toward the ceiling and floated toward the center of the room for a simple demonstration. Power was present to do more than that, but it was power under control. Flying or levitating in this room, although a minimal expression thereof, was a challenge to the beliefs of some present in the room. You can't drive a six-ton truck over a two-ton bridge! This demonstration of power was encouraging to the other folks to have faith to fly.

Typically in the flying genre of dreams, I am encouraging the Terrestrials to believe that they can also fly. It is a sign of the anointing (i.e., power) of the Spirit. I've had various types of flying dreams in the context of ministry meetings, where individuals deny the power of the Holy Spirit to work miracles today. In the dreams, these Cessationists (who deny the current power of the Holy Spirit to work miracles) point at me and say derogatory remarks about the "inappropriateness" of flying or levitating. They errantly presume that anything miraculous, like flying or levitating, must be of the devil or laden with witchcraft. Funny thing is, that's precisely what the religious leaders accused Jesus of doing two millennia ago when he worked miracles.

In another flying dream I was floating inside a tall building at ca. 70 feet elevation and singing the chorus of the secular tune – *"I believe I can fly"* (see below). As I sang this tune, a heavenly chorus joined me, albeit in a heavenly language. It was in perfect harmony with my English lyrics, but altogether supernatural. Then, my daughter Catherine, the former skydiver, looked upward at me from the floor. I encouraged her and she joined me in flight nearby, but a little bit below me. She was concentrating with her eyes closed on flying trusting the Spirit to guide her. I was helping train her in flying. But, when I spoke to her it broke her concentration. She opened her eyes and fell down part of the way.

Each of us must know our own level of faith. We must not presumptuously take people too far too fast on their own journey of faith. Remember a six-ton truck will collapse a two-ton bridge. Laura and I have great expectations for each of our four children. We expect great things from our Great God on their behalf. Catherine was born to *soar on eagle's wings* with an otherworldly and prescient perspective (see Isaiah 40:31). So, in honor of my remarkable daughter, Catherine, I present the chorus to the song *"I Believe I Can Fly"* by R. Kelly:

> *I believe I can fly*
> *I believe I can touch the sky*
> *I think about it every night and day*
> *Spread my wings and fly away*
> *I believe I can soar*
> *I see me running through that open door*
> *I believe I can fly*

4
STRUGGLES AGAINST INJUSTICE

"The Spirit of the Lord is on me, because he has anointed me to preach good news to the poor. He has sent me to proclaim freedom for the prisoners and recovery of sight for the blind, to release the oppressed, to proclaim the year of the Lord's favor."

~ Luke 4:18-19; Isaiah 61:1-2

OPPRESSION IN THE SOUTH

Colonel Stone Johnson was a "foot soldier" in the Civil Rights Movement in Birmingham, Alabama starting in 1954. He was living in the prejudiced and racist Southeastern USA, and served as a personal aide and bodyguard to some of the Civil Rights leaders, such as Fred Shuttlesworth and Martin Luther King, Jr.

Colonel Johnson and I first became acquaintances when he graciously gave a personal tour of the Civil Rights Institute of Birmingham to a foreign diplomat from the Kenyan Embassy, who was my guest. After completing this special tour, Colonel Johnson expressed a life-long desire to visit Africa at least once in his lifetime. So, Path Clearer ministries flew 87-year-old Mr. Johnson as my traveling companion to Nigeria in 2005. While there, we participated in the world's largest assembly of millions of people, to fulfill the goal by Colonel Stone Johnson to see Africa. King David wrote, *"Delight yourself in the Lord and he will give you the desires of your heart."* (Psalm 37:4); and *"May he give you the desire of your heart and make all your plans succeed."* (Psalm 20:4).

Colonel Johnson was intimately involved in actions of courage in addressing the needs of the poor blacks of Alabama. He was a bi-vocational servant leader. He worked a full-time job to provide for his family, but then devoted the remainder of his time to helping the Civil Rights Movement and in his local church. He and an associate personally removed a "live" bomb inside of a bucket that was positioned next to a church facility. Moments later the bomb exploded in the street. There were so many bombing incidents against black leaders of the Civil Rights Movement in Birmingham that the city was nicknamed "Bombingham". Some of you will recall the bombing deaths of four little girls at the Sixteenth Street Baptist Church. That heinous incident helped to crystallize public outrage against the racial prejudice and injustice that was so deeply engrained and tolerated by the whites in the Deep South.

Colonel Stone Johnson is a righteous man, filled with the Father's love for all of God's creation. He stood in the gap on behalf of others, who either could not or would not take a stand against racial injustices. I admire the courage of men like Colonel Stone Johnson and Fred Shuttlesworth (whom coincidentally I've also met), as well as Ralph Abernathy and Martin Luther King, Jr. The latter in particular was a "prophet" of that season. I firmly believe that ML King was more of a prophet than he was a "Civil Rights worker". He was the "voice" chosen for that pivotal season. The voices and actions of him and his co-laborers helped to stir awareness of racial injustices, which were supported by the systems of the ruling government at the local and state level. They fought for the *Voting Rights Act* and for equal access to employment and to public facilities. They also fought for recognition of African-Americans as "fully" human, as absurd as that biased perspective might seem in retrospect from today's vantage point. Oh! How quickly we forget our past. We would rather just be comfortable and sweep all unpleasant memories aside.

The Civil Rights leaders were the sentinel lightning rods of reproach, because of their desires to generate hope amongst the hopeless! The campaign to defeat hopelessness was hard fought in Alabama and other Southern states. This desire was encapsulated within the momentous conclusion of Dr. King's famous "I Have a Dream" speech on The Mall in Washington, DC. As a prophet of his day, he cast a vision of hope for those needing to see the promise of a better day ahead:

> *"...I say to you today, my friends, so even though we face the difficulties of today and tomorrow, I still have a dream. It is a dream deeply rooted in the*

American dream. I have a dream that one day this nation will rise up and live out the true meaning of its creed: 'We hold these truths to be self-evident: that all men are created equal.' I have a dream that one day on the red hills of Georgia the sons of former slaves and the sons of former slave owners will be able to sit down together at the table of brotherhood. I have a dream that one day even the state of Mississippi, a state sweltering with the heat of injustice, sweltering with the heat of oppression, will be transformed into an oasis of freedom and justice. I have a dream that my four little children will one day live in a nation where they will not be judged by the color of their skin but by the content of their character. I have a dream today. I have a dream that one day, down in Alabama, with its vicious racists, with its governor having his lips dripping with the words of interposition and nullification; one day right there in Alabama, little black boys and black girls will be able to join hands with little white boys and white girls as sisters and brothers. I have a dream today. I have a dream that one day every valley shall be exalted, every hill and mountain shall be made low, the rough places will be made plain, and the crooked places will be made straight, and the glory of the Lord shall be revealed, and all flesh shall see it together. This is our hope. This is the faith that I go back to the South with. With this faith we will be able to hew out of the mountain of despair a stone of hope. With this faith we will be able to transform the jangling discords of our nation into a beautiful symphony of brotherhood. With this faith we will be able to work together, to pray together, to struggle together, to go to jail together, to stand up for freedom together, knowing that we will be free one day. This will be the day when all of God's children will be able to sing with a new meaning, 'My country, 'tis of thee, sweet land of liberty, of thee I sing. Land where my fathers died, land of the pilgrim's pride, from every mountainside, let freedom ring.' And if America is to be a great nation this must become true. So let freedom ring from the prodigious hilltops of New Hampshire. Let freedom ring from the mighty mountains of New York. Let freedom ring from the heightening Alleghenies of Pennsylvania! Let freedom ring from the snowcapped Rockies of Colorado! Let freedom ring from the curvaceous slopes of California! But not only that; let freedom ring from Stone Mountain of Georgia! Let freedom ring from Lookout Mountain of Tennessee! Let freedom ring from every hill and molehill of Mississippi. From every mountainside, let freedom ring. And when this happens, When we allow freedom to ring, when we let

---

it ring from every village and every hamlet, from every state and every city, we will be able to speed up that day when all of God's children, black men and white men, Jews and Gentiles, Protestants and Catholics, will be able to join hands and sing in the words of the old Negro spiritual, 'Free at last! Free at last! Thank God Almighty, we are free at last!'"

BEREA COLLEGE

During the mid-19th Century slave ownership was commonplace in the plantations and farmlands of the Southeastern states of America. But, in Berea, a small Kentucky town, children of financially disadvantaged families were given an opportunity to obtain a higher education. To this day Berea College has had an exceptional altruistic vision and produces well-trained college graduates.

It is an exclusive environment. But, not in the way that one might expect. Ironically, students from affluent families are not even permitted to attend their classes. The college caters only to those who have limited financial means, many from poor black or white homes in the Appalachian Mountains.

The college was founded by John G. Fee six years before the infamous Civil War. He and other staunch abolitionist Christians wanted to compensate for the disparity between the *haves* and the *have-nots*. They wanted an environment that was open to all poor students regardless of race or gender. This was not a trendy philosophy in those days, and especially in Kentucky and other Southern states. In fact, John Fee and his associates at Berea College faced fierce opposition, enduring multiple severe beatings, threats to their lives, and even being exiled from the state for a period of years. Yet they returned and persisted, weathering social, legislative, and economic difficulties. Their Biblical values stirred concern for the less fortunate and a calling *"to preach and apply a gospel of impartial love."* To this day, those values continue to guide Berea College's work.

An administrator at the college, Jeff Blake, shared with me that God has richly blessed this college with a phenomenal endowment that enables Berea College to underwrite approximately three fourths of the costs for all of their students' tuition and expenses. In today's terms that is equivalent to an $80,000 scholarship for each of the 1,500 students. The remainder is obtained from other sources, so that none of the students need pay anything to attend. Truly remarkable!

I thank God for the legacy of Christian righteousness and charity in the hearts of Berea College's founder and current leadership. This is a profound example to the world of Heaven invading Earth – the Kingdom of God invading the kingdoms of men. It is a prescient picture of what the future Millennial reign of Jesus Christ might resemble, when He will rule the nations with a rod-of-iron, with truth-in-love, and will compensate for the egregious sinful disparities of the past. Berea College is an image of the best that man can do aided by the favor of God.

STRUGGLING UNDER OPPRESSIVE GOVERNMENTS IN EUROPE

Peter Dugulescu was a young married Baptist pastor in Romania during the days of Communist control. Under the dictatorial oppression of the Coucescu regime the local churches were scrutinized and controlled by communist government infiltrators. Peter experienced great difficulties as he sought to obey the calling that he had received from the Lord, after he became a "repenter" and follower of Jesus. His life was threatened multiple times, and these were not idle threats. He was once driving his car when a bus was intentionally crashed into the side of his door to attempt to kill him. To this day there is still clear evidence of that accident. He has misaligned bones in his arm. On another occasion Peter was intentionally poisoned and deprived of humane care while in the hospital. His family endured persistent uncertainties of whether he would survive the onslaught. It was very taxing on the entire family as he persisted in obedience to the Lord of Hosts.

As a pastor of a local congregation that was preaching and teaching Biblical truths, he had become an "enemy" of the state. The officials dictated either agnostic/atheistic philosophy or a cozy syncretic tolerance of the Eastern Orthodox leadership, who were heavily influenced by the government. But, there was no room for genuine Disciples of Christ in Romania. There was no room for any freedom of expression.

As President Thomas Jefferson declared, *"Resistance to tyrants is obedience to God."* At the critical juncture in time, a *kairos* moment, when communism's chokehold was about to break, Pastor Dugulescu volunteered to address an outdoor large public assembly near the opera house in Timosoira, Romania. He courageously placed his life on the line to lead his nation in public prayer. The communist government lost its stranglehold during that critical week. He eventually was elected to serve in the Parliament, the first "protestant" to be honored in this manner. His remarkable story is recorded in his autobiography, <u>Repenters</u>. That is the term given to a genuine believer in Romania, because without repentance no one can be saved. It is easy to be called a "Christian", but to be called a "Repenter" meant you had really chosen to become an obedient child of God. It was a costly distinction.

I've spent some time with Peter on several occasions. He is a passionate voice for Jesus within his nation. In spite of years of persecution, he is not bitter. He has a loving spirit and a scintillating personality. At present he helps orphans and the elderly with food, clothing, and shelter. He breathes hope into those he encounters around the globe.

1939 – A PIVOTAL YEAR:

The year 1939 was a year of infamy. It was the year that anti-Semitic *rhetoric* boiled over the edges of a heated cauldron of hatred and became *reality* within Europe. Caustic words catalyzed caustic actions. For the prior seven years, Adolf Hilter and his SS leaders spewed the stench of virulent anti-Semitism throughout Germany and Austria. They considered Jews (Juden) to be sub-human vermin and worthy of annihilation. From the early 1930's until 1945, Hitler's regime devised and implemented the "Final Solution" to the "Jewish Problem" – the systematic murder of all Jews in Germany and the occupied lands. It was a masterful plan.

The stench of Hitler's hate-filled words ultimately led to the gas chambers of Auschwitz, into which 1.5 million human bodies were asphyxiated by Zyklon B gas canisters that released cyanide gas. The bodies of men, women, and children were subsequently taken to high efficiency disassembly and incineration lines. Many of them were killed on the very day that the rail cars arrived from elsewhere in Europe and unloaded them at the "Selection Point". Those "fortunate" enough to not be selected for immediate gassing were subjected to inhumane conditions of forced labor, insufficient food, lice, lack of clothing, and myriad other tortures. The "fortunate" typically lasted only a few months under these conditions before they too were incinerated. This stench of German xenophobia and oppression led to an estimated 6 million Jewish deaths alone by an intelligent, systematic, and technological murdering machine. This was the European Holocaust.

1939 was the year of Poland's humiliation at the hands of invaders. From 1939 until 1945 Poland became the *waste dump* of evil coming out of Germany and also Russia, although the latter is seldom known by Westerners. Poland was squeezed between two enemy nations. Polish citizens were over-run and annihilated from the East and from the West. This crisis ultimately led to numerous German "concentration camps" in Poland, of which Auschwitz was among the most notorious.

In 2006 I took a Path Clearer team from the US and UK into Poland for a ministry trip entitled "Piercing the Darkness Over Europe". While there, we visited the infamous Warsaw Ghetto district and the Auschwitz death camp, for the purpose of opposing the current rise of anti-Semitism and neo-Nazism in Europe. We learned a small measure about the atrocities of Poland's dark historic past. But, while we were in Warsaw we worshiped, prayed, and danced while singing "Baruch Hashem Adonai", which is Hebrew for "Blessed be the name of the Lord". We stood in memory and solidarity with those who had suffered in the past under the oppression of the German and Russian oppressors. We also declared blessings over Poland's believers and nation.

We pierced the darkness in many cities, even within the Brandenburg Gate in Berlin. After visiting Poland and Berlin we then ministered in Neustadt-Glewe, in what was formerly East Germany. We finally arrived in the Netherlands, where we toured the home of Corey ten Boom in Haarlem, who was the author of <u>The Hiding Place</u>. In May 1940 the German Wehrmacht army (i.e., the regular army) and the Waffen SS (i.e., the "Nazi" political army) invaded Holland, as Hitler established a broad footprint over Europe and Northern Africa.

Cory and the entire ten Boom family were active participants in the underground Resistance Movement opposing the Germans' plans to arrest Jewish people for deportation. There was a long-term prophetic mantle of intercession for the Jews and the future nation of Israel (in

—

45

1948) upon this Christian family since 1844. Yes, for an entire century the family held regular prayer meetings for Jews and Israel. Those prayers paved the way for God to use this family in the Resistance Movement in order to help Jewish people during 1943 and 1944 in the city of Haarlem. One of the tools they used to assist various Jews was a "hiding place" consisting of a small narrow space behind a false wall that they had constructed and disguised.

The family's role in protecting and providing for Jews was discovered. Corey and her sister, Betsy, were eventually arrested by the German occupiers for their roles in aiding the Jews in Haarlem. Not only did the inevitable happen, but, Corey had received a prophetic vision of warning at the time of the German invasion of Holland about being taken captive in the future by the Germans. In her biography she wrote, *"And it was then that I had the dream. It couldn't have been a real dream because I was not asleep. But a scene was suddenly and unreasonably in my mind. I saw the Grote Markt, half a block away, as clearly as though I were standing there, saw the town hall and St. Bavo's and the fish mart with its stair-stepped façade. Then as I watched, a kind of odd, old farm wagon – old fashioned and out of place in the middle of a city – came lumbering across the square pulled by four enormous black horses. To my surprise I saw that I myself was sitting in the wagon. And Father too! And Betsie! There were many others, some strangers, some friends. I recognized Pickwick and Toos, Willem and young Peter. All together we were slowly being drawn across the square behind those horses. We couldn't get off the wagon, that was the terrible thing. It was taking us away – far away, I felt – but we didn't want to go…"* [The Hiding Place, Corey ten Boom, p.62].

Corey's vision was repeated later, *"And then an extraordinary thing happened. Even as I prayed, that waking dream passed again before my eyes. I saw again those four black horses and the Grote Markt. As I had on the night of the invasion I scanned the passengers drawn so unwillingly behind them. Father, Betsie, Willem, myself – leaving Haarlem, leaving all that was sure and safe – going where?"* [ibid., p. 74]. After her immediate family was arrested in a remarkably similar manner to the vision the biography continues: *"Then I recalled. The vision. The night of the invasion. I had seen it all. Willem, Nollie, Pickwick, Peter – all of us here – drawn against our wills across this square. It had all been in the dream – all of us leaving Haarlem, unable to turn back. Going where?"* [ibid., p. 135-136.] God in his graciousness had given to Corey a glimpse of the grim season ahead. Even a cursory reading of the prophets of the Scriptures indicates that God often reveals warnings of future dangers through his seers and prophetic individuals. He still does to this current day! Corey had been shown rhema revelation to help warn and prepare for her family's future.

This Dutch Christian family had prayed for Jews for a century and now they stood in solidarity with the Jews who were being deported to almost certain deaths. The sisters were sent to Scheveningen prison and eventually ended up in Ravensbruck concentration camp, where they were used as forced laborers and badly mistreated. Corey ten Boom recalled their treatment in prison as excruciatingly terrible. There was starvation, infestations by pests, cruel beatings, forced labor, and innumerable inhumane acts against the prisoners by their captors.

Her beloved sister Besty died in the camp in December 1944. Shortly thereafter Corey was released from the concentration camp, due to a clerical mistake, which was a sovereign blessing from the Almighty. She forgave the Germans who abused her and Betsy and murdered members of her family. Corey shared the love of Jesus with fellow prisoners and after her release around the globe until her death in 1983. She was an incredible courageous servant of the Most High! Corey Ten Boom fulfilled a prophetic destiny that had begun a century before by her ancestors, who had interceded on behalf of the apple of God's eye, the Jewish people, through whom the Savior of the world had come.

But, lest we forget the great Holocaust of Europe was not the *only* holocaust to have blemished the earth. There have been many holocausts. For instance, an estimated 70 million died under the Maoist regime of China between the late 1930's and 1980's. And some historians speculate that there might have been an equal or greater loss of life among the First Nations Peoples of the Americas.

OPPRESSION OF FIRST NATIONS PEOPLES

Tragedy upon tragedy befell the Native American "Nations" who occupied North America prior to the arrival of European traders and settlers. They were the true First Nations Peoples entrusted for millennia with the care of the land. They did a fine job as custodians or stewards of the land, and without any help from the European colonizers. Annexation under the errant philosophy of "Manifest Destiny" eventually displaced them from all but a tiny portion of the lands of North America. Today only a few percentage of all of the landmass of the USA and Canada remains set apart for use by Native Americans. Friends, this is not right.

The loss of historically implied or contractual territorial "rights" by the original occupiers was accomplished through a sequence of hundreds of violated treaties offered by government officials. In many cases it is questionable whether the "white" settlers ever intended to honor the contractual terms of the treaties, and in other cases likely resulted from a measure of intimidation by the white settlers. Many Europeans found it convenient to overlook their own responsibilities to honor their word, in view of their personal gains in these lucrative lopsided transactions.

Simply said, the white man's word was virtually worthless. And, after several hundred years many Native Americans harbor much-deserved mistrust toward white men. Jesus said, *"By their fruit you will recognize them."* (Matthew 7:16a). Sadly much of the fruit is rotten. Words are cheap; actions speak loudly. The book of James provides clear admonition to believers to speak the truth and to honor one's word. For centuries self-declared Catholic and Protestant "Christians" failed to honor the First Nations Peoples by keeping their word. Scripture says clearly that it is better to not pledge than to pledge and not pay.

Descendents of North Europeans, like myself, are indebted to our Native American citizens. We have directly and indirectly benefited at the loss to their ancestors. Many of the consequences of those dishonest words and actions are still in effect today. It is further compounded by less than honest treatment in our history books, many of which have been prepared from the following biases:

- "Aren't the Christians supposed to convert the 'heathens'?"
- "Isn't *Manifest Destiny* what God intended for the Americas?"
- "Doesn't the end justify the means? Oh, just look at the great outcome!"
- "Weren't the Founding Fathers inspired by God during colonization and expansion toward the West?"

If you were to become familiar with a few Native Americans, and you made those remarks to them…Whew! Get out the fire extinguisher and blow it on your burning ears before they turn to crispy potato chips! He who writes history books writes history, and it isn't always 'right'. To the victor go the spoils.

In recent years I have begun to research and appreciate the deep-seated "pain" and sense of conflict in the thoughts of Native Americans. Not that I know much about it by experience at this juncture, but I have intentionally begun to learn through new friendships with Native Americans. Through books written by Native American ministers, such as Richard Twiss (Lakota Souix) and Randy Woodley (Cherokee) among others, I have begun to understand a little about their collective pain. Yet these individuals are not seeking pity. They have much to offer, and not only to those within the Native American communities, but, also to those of other non-Native cultures around the globe.

Unfortunately, the "elitist" views of North European descendents still hinder understanding of the great value of Native American cultural and societal expressions. The North European settlers enforced practices upon First Nations Peoples that denied the validity and richness of their cultures, dress and hair styles, educational models, languages, and philosophies of life. The Native American emphases on relationships of trust, honor for elders, harmony between the spiritual and physical realms, and passionate "free" expressions of worship of the Creator as a way-of-life are among their many wonderful and Biblically consistent values. They can be excellent teachers to those of us who are not Native Americans, if we'll resist the all-to-natural temptation to believe that our understanding of "Judeo-Christian" values and practices is superior in illumination and/or mutually exclusive relative to those of Native Americans. Many, if not most, of us have a long way to go in understanding, appreciation, and learning about our First Nations Peoples. Let us become a new generation of learners. Let's resist the temptation to "tell them" without reciprocity. Rather, let's first honor them by sitting at their feet and walking a mile in their moccasins. Let's reserve making quick conclusions based upon our Western-biased model of spirituality. Although it will be a challenge to many of us, let's simply listen first to their wisdom and counsel. Cross-cultural dialogue is not always easy. We can chew on the chicken and later spit out the bones.

One of the many absurdities dumped upon the Native Americans during the conquests of the North Europeans was a particular North European *form* of the religion of Chrisitanity. A high proportion of the settlers to the "New World" were in fact believers in Jesus. But, in ignorance they imported a style or form of Christianity that imparted an elitist view of understanding. It wasn't simply good enough to present *Jesus-the-Creator-Son* from the pages of the Scriptures. It wasn't just presenting the substance of Jesus as God's radiant holy Son, it was all bogged down in the "religion" of Western Christianity. This imposed system of religion carried with it all manner of denominational doctrines (many conflicting one another). There were ceremonies and religious symbols and clothing. Many of these "things" had little if anything to do with explicit Biblical revelation of the Truth. Many were just Western (i.e., Greco-Roman rational) expressions of man-made religious practices. We are often ignorant of the powerful influence of our own biases.

Let us not confuse the person and truths of the Creator-Son revealed in the Scriptures and our chosen religious practices and rituals. There is an abundance of cultural expressions of Christianity worldwide. These are man's attempts to comprehend the Creator's desires for worship and service. They don't necessarily follow a single template. To one race or tribe worship is manifest in one form, but in another race or tribe worship is manifest in another form. Provided the chosen form is not in direct conflict with Scripture, we should consider Paul's admonition to the Jewish believers to not impose their religious traditions and laws upon the Gentiles in the book of Acts. All is permissible (albeit provided it doesn't violate Scripture), but not all is profitable. Jesus also admonished his followers that if a man is not *against* you, he is *for* you. Therefore, leave him alone (see Mark 9:38-41). The Kingdom of God has vast breadth. It cannot be confined by the views of a single denomination, or race, or tribe as to what is acceptable or normative behavior. Unless explicitly forbidden by Scripture, let us learn to embrace the diversity of expressions of worship.

In this context my friend Don Stewart recommended to me the wisdom of E. Stanley Jones, a successful evangelist in India, recorded in a book published in 1925. Note that India in his text is located in the Asian subcontinent and does not concern American Indians *per se.*

Nonetheless, Mr. Jones wrote concerning the tendency toward Christian religion's cultural myopia:

> *"If some are afraid of what might happen if we were to give India Jesus without hard-and-fast systems of thought and ecclesiastical organization, lest the whole be corrupted, let our fears be allayed. Jesus is well able to take care of himself. He trusted himself to the early disciples, who were no better and no worse than the Indian people; and having got hold of him they went forth in that name with power. Having little ecclesiastical system, little body of set doctrine, they created their own forms out of the passion of love they had for him. These forms were real because they came out of the white heat of that passion. They expressed life. We believe that India will fall intensely in love with the Christ of the Indian Road, that love will turn to glad submission to him as Saviour and Lord, that out of that loving submission will come a new radiant expression of him in thought and life. We who feel that we must be steadiers of the ark must remember that Jesus can take care of himself, even in moments when there seems most to fear."* [The Christ of the Indian Road, E. Stanley Jones, Abingdon Press, New York, 1925, p. 175.]

Had the Christian settlers from England and Europe who met the Indians of India or the "Indians" of North America focused more on the divine person of Jesus and less on the religious practices of Christianity, the Gospel may well have exploded exponentially in short order in both places. Had our founding fathers focused more on the power and love of the Holy Spirit and manifested in their lives, and less upon the creeds and knowledge-for-knowledge sake which Westerner's crave, it is safe to speculate that Native Americans would have quickly embraced the saving knowledge of their Creator expressed through Jesus.

The First Nations Peoples' receptivity to the Gospel was hindered by the oppressive manner in which it was declared to them. The white man's focus was on "destroying Indian culture" in order to "save the Indian". It was an utter failure! It was disgraceful. *"...A crushed spirit dries up the bones."* (Proverbs 17:22b). The ill-advised strategy crushed the hopes and dreams of Native Americans. The fruit of this historic crushing blow is still seen today on reservations, where teen suicide runs rampant, substance abuse is common to numb the pain and hopelessness, and individuals struggle with their self-identity and depression. None of these problems were common before the North European annexation of Native lands. Yet, had the Westerners built genuine relationships of trust and enquired with open minds and hearts about the worship practices and traditions of the Native Americans, they would have been surprised at some of the commonalities present in both. But, few sought common ground. It was just easier to "lord it over" the Indians and move forward with expansion into their territories. And, all the while many white pioneers and settlers did so with the confidence that the hand of God was upon them…how ironic.

Oh! How history unfortunately repeats itself. A valuable lesson could have been learned from a contemporary, who was working in a cross-cultural manner during the 19th Century in another continent. By examining the cross-cultural awareness of Hudson Taylor in China, key insights could have been gained. He was a physician-missionary from England who decided that the cultural norms of local society could either serve to help or to hinder the advance of the Gospel. If one simply replaced the English style of dress and the length of one's hair, it became much easier to present the Good News to a ready audience in China. However, it came at a high cost to him personally, but not from the Chinese. He was ill treated by his fellow British and European colleagues, who considered his behavior distasteful, questionable, and undignified. They thought he was stooping to sub-standard treatment of Christian heritage, when in fact Hudson correctly discerned the difference between cultural norms and the recorded Word of God. Dr. Taylor was not a slave to the *spirit of religion*. Oh, it is my desire to see the captives of the demonic *spirit of religion* set free!

I have been particularly fond of Mr. Taylor since I first read his biography in the late 1980's while living in London. I've had the privilege of visiting key sites in England connected to Hudson Taylor. My family once lived just north from where he once lived in East London. I worked at the Imperial Cancer Research Fund on Lincoln's Inn next to the Royal College of Surgeons, where he studied medicine. I have been inside of the Royal College on several occasions. And, I've knelt down and prayed on the docks of Liverpool giving honor to the hardest day of his life – the day he bid farewell to his grieving mother in September of 1853, as he sailed out the Mersey River on his initial voyage of faith toward China. I, too, have shed tears on the banks of the Mersey. Not tears of sadness, but of honor where honor is due. And, those were tears of blessing for God's present purposes for China.

Hudson Taylor understood the value of cultural adaptations. Unfortunately few "Christian" settlers to North America followed his wisdom in regard to their presentation of the Gospel to the Native Americans. Oh, had they followed the empowering principle, *"Christ above religion!"* But, instead they imposed an elitist Western form of so-called Christianity, and decimated any inherent truth in the spirituality of First Nations Peoples' cultures and traditions, without even seeking to identify the numerous "redemptive" components of these practices. God had given some revelation to the First Nations Peoples, and our forefathers barely attempted to give any notice.

However, not all white men were hostile toward Native Americans. I am pleased to say that my own Great Grandfather George Schuetz (born in 1880) was a trusted friend of the Kickapoo, who were displaced to Brown County in Northeastern Kansas from Illinois. A few years ago at night the "Voice" of the Lord informed me to *"Ask your mother about her grandfather, the Indian."* I didn't know that information in the natural, as I had performed genealogical research on my family and knew that my great grandfather was from a German lineage. So, the next day I contacted my mother and she informed me that her grandfather had been a man of integrity with whom the Kickapoo had a friendly relationship of trust. He even danced with them in worship and dance celebrations in Indian regalia, which was likely rare for a white man.

This night-time revelation about my great grandfather plus several other dreams with Native American themes birthed a desire within me to contact the Kickapoo Nation's leadership, so as to become a blessing to them. However, I knew that they would be aware of the need for me to honor their cultural *protocol* that dictated that I could not invite myself directly to meet with them. I would need to honor the protocol established of the Spirit, and they would have to invite me as an unknown visitor, as highly improbable as that was. But, I didn't know a single Kickapoo, even though I had lived the early days of my life not far from their reservation. So, I sought to make contact through a "go-between" person, with whom they might be familiar. None were found. So, I prayed the prayer of faith for the door to open in spite of the difficult circumstances. I had done all that I could do and still honor their protocol. Amazingly, the Creator had sovereignly arranged for my former best friend from 7th to 10th grades, Chris Thompson of Creek Indian heritage, to be "adopted" as a Kickapoo. This adoption had recently happened without my knowledge. Through Chris, the Creator has opened a "new" door. I have begun the journey of becoming familiar with and a blessing to the Kickapoo. May the Creator grant special blessings of His favor upon the Kickapoo Nation and their relatives in Oklahoma, Texas, and Mexico.

WILLIAM PENN

While dismal treatment of Native Americans by European settlers has been commonplace since the 16th Century, one striking example of honor to the contrary was William Penn. From the Native American perspective today, there weren't many European colonizers who were honorable. Yet, in Penn we find a glimmer of hope and a man of substance. I recommend <u>The Seed of a Nation: Rediscovering America</u> by Darrell Fields, for information about Penn's honorable life in relationship to the Native Americans.

It is a difficult and intentional process to be "loosed" from the limitations of one's cultural blinders of nationality, heritage, and race. William Penn was a British aristocrat whose family was granted by the British government a large territory in the newly evolving Colonies, as repayment for a debt to the Crown. [For the sake of staying "on message", I will not venture to address whether the British government was entitled to that land on the West Coast of the Atlantic.]

Mr. Penn was a pious and God-conscious man. He was a Quaker. Although the privileges of affluence and the position of governance and honor were bestowed upon him, he intentionally sought understanding and mutually beneficial relationship with the Native American tribes in the Northeastern territories. He understood the value of building relationships of trust and loyalty, which sadly were often set aside with ease by his colleagues. Please note this as a fact – relationships and binding covenants that are honored are highly esteemed by Native Americans. In contrast in the white man's culture, relationships are often temporary and covenants are easily overlooked and denied out of convenience. All to often the "covenants" of white men are not really covenants, they're just words that can be abandoned if it suits the individual's interests. But, this is not consistent with Native American spirituality or social structure.

Altruism can be defined as good intentions and actions for the benefit of others, without regard for one's self. Altruism is a core value of First Nations culture(s). But, to many white men altruism is a burden too inconvenient to carry. The modern mantra *"What's in it for me?"* (WIFM) has sunk its talons into the flesh of many selfish people. I, for one, am on a mission to see altruism restored among the followers of The Way. I even founded a company by the name ALtruis. I am convinced that genuine "significance" in life is found in altruism and in relationships. Significance is not found in personal accomplishments or accumulation of assets, rather in blessing other people. Jesus came to be a servant and as a sacrifice for others. His life was filled with significance. Jesus was an altruist! Significance in life is proportional to maintaining the three relationships of highest priority...those being *faith, family, and friends.*

Penn's faith in the Creator and understanding of the First Nations Peoples was exceptional *vis-à-vis* his peer group. Through the 20-20 hindsight of perspective today, we could criticize many things about William Penn's motives and actions as a participant in colonization of the First Nations lands. We all walk in seasons of historical and relative blindness. However, within the context of his day, Penn was a remarkable man of compassionate understanding and altruism. He sought peaceful co-existence with the Native Americans. Yet the colonial selfish interests of the British and French governments were leading to warfare on the advancing Western front. Native Americans were betrayed, lied to, and "used" for the colonial agendas of foreigners. These forces of greed and warfare were greater than the reach of one honorable man, William Penn. But, I do honor him.

In conclusion, what would have happened if the leaders of the Civil Rights Movement or Berea College had chosen less challenging paths and not fulfilled their roles in destiny? What would have happened if no one stood up against the Communists in Romania or the Nazis invading from

Germany? What if there had never been a Colonel Stone Johnson, or a John G. Fee, or a Peter Dugulescu, or a Corey ten Boom, or a William Penn? The courageous actions of these individuals in the face of oppressive government officials made a difference then. And, their legacy still benefits their fellow men and women today. You can take this message to the bank – It doesn't take an entire village to generate hope, it only takes one person committed to living a gospel of truth-in-love.

5

FOR CRYING OUT LOUD!

A voice of one calling: "In the desert prepare the way for the LORD;
make straight in the wilderness a highway for our God. Every valley shall be raised up,
every mountain and hill made low; the rough ground shall become level, the rugged places a
plain. And the glory of the LORD will be revealed, and all mankind together will see it.
For the mouth of the LORD has spoken."
A voice says, "Cry out." And I said, "What shall I cry?"

~ Isaiah 40:3-6a

One of the often-overlooked keys to restoring hope within the Kingdom of God is found in the spiritual gift of prophecy. Contemporary prophecy can identify the root causes of problems. It can reveal in the light things formerly hidden in darkness. And, it can provide much-needed encouragement at a time of doubt or pain.

This spiritual gift of special revelation is very dynamic with many manifestations. For instance, prophecy can range from subtle promptings of the Holy Spirit to vivid graphic dreams and visions, some of which deal with events in the past or future. Another manifestation of this spiritual gift is to make declarations that bring alignment to the truth and restoration to the wayward. John-the-baptizer was a profound example of a prophet of the latter type, who exhorted people to recognize and live in the truth.

John-the-baptizer was a prophetic voice crying in the wilderness. He was chosen while yet in the womb as the oracle for God's *greatest* message ever, the soon-to-come Kingdom of the Creator-Son on earth (similar to Jeremiah 1:5). He spoke hope and life into the barrenness of Israel while under Roman, Herodian, and Sanhedrin dominion. He spoke from the lowest ranks of man to the highest of rulers in the region. He spoke to those who had ears to hear, as well as to those who rejected his message. He even rebuked the Herodian quasi-Jewish leader of his day for personal sin…and it landed him in jail.

John was the real deal, an obedient prophet. He knew well the mean-ing of, *"for crying out loud"*. Jesus spoke of him in a superlative term as the "greatest" of all men to walk the earth. *"The greatest man to ever live"* was John, the desert-dwelling prophet, who ate locusts and wild honey. Ironi-cally, the life of a genuine prophet often produces harsh criticism and frequent rejection. Even Jesus noted about himself as a prophet, *"They hated me without reason."* (John 15:25b). Rejection and criticism are com-mon burdens that a prophet must bear. The pains of rejection must be processed in order to build up the character of a prophet.

A lot of people walking in darkness would rather remain in the dark-ness (see John 3:19-20). Light is painful to them. Light exposes the con-dition of their heart. Light reveals the ugliness of sin and thus stimulates godly guilt, shame, and remorse. John the Baptist's courageous words literally cost him his head. And it wasn't because he spoke something *nice* to a ruler that he was martyred. He died in obedience because he spoke the truth-in-love.

I believe it is God's desire that all believers develop the ability to prophesy. Moses said, *"I wish that all the Lord's people were prophets and that the Lord would put his Spirit on them!"* (Numbers 11:29; emphasis added). Paul admonishes that we should all desire spiritual gifts and *especially* the gift of prophecy (see 1 Corinthians 14:1-5). Contemporary prophecy was an essential integral component of the 1ˢᵗ Century Church, and should be in our days as well. The Lord has always had a remnant of prophets and prophetic voices during each season of time. Just one of many examples of a Christian prophet from the intervening period was Alexander Peden of Scotland, during the 17ᵗʰ Century Reformation. There have been true prophets in the days before, during, and after Jesus' dwelling on earth. There are still true prophets today.

The prophets of old were admonished to speak *whatever* God told them. An obedient prophet can't pick and choose what he or she desires to speak on behalf of the Lord. The prophet Jeremiah provides many instances of rebuking the all-too-common false prophets, who *only* spoke pleasant words and blessings. Prophets hear warnings and cautions, in addition to pleasant things. Ezekiel 3, 22, and 33 indicate that prophet-ic watchmen are accountable for not only perceiving warnings, but also sharing them with others. Their job is to be a voice *"for crying out loud!"*

Let us digress for a moment. There once was a prophet, who received stock tips from God. Knowing that the Holy Spirit had given the prophet a special spiritual gift of divine revelation, he decided to capitalize on it. He interviewed for a job at a stock brokerage firm. During the interview the boss asked him why he felt that he was qualified for the job as a stockbroker, even though he had neither university coursework nor training in finance. He replied, *"You're right, I don't know much about this field. But, I'm a prophet and God speaks to me. He tells me which stocks to buy and when to buy them."* The boss was surprised and impressed. So, he hired the fellow on the spot thinking the firm could turn a quick *profit* from the stock-picking *prophet!*

Six months later the supervisor looked over several written complaints filed by the prophet's clients. That forced the manager to review the account transaction reports for the new employee's job performance. The manager was shocked to see that none of the clients had made any money from the prophet's "insider trading" information. So, in a panic the manager called the prophet into his office to chastise him. The boss screamed, *"When I hired you, didn't you tell me that God tells you which stocks to buy and when to buy them?"* The humble prophet replied, *"Yes sir. God does tell me that information."* This response angered the manager, so he probed further, *"Then, why in the world aren't your clients making any money? They're calling our firm disappointed with their accounts."* So, the prophet replied, *"When you hired me I told you that God tells me which stocks to buy and when to buy them. But, He hasn't chosen to tell me which stocks to sell and when to sell them!"*

The moral of the story is, *"We know in part, and prophecy in part"* (1 Corinthians 13:9). Contemporary prophets and prophetic people are not perfect, even though some (and hopefully the vast majority) of what they receive is on target. They make mistakes (refer to <u>Praying Faith</u> for more on this topic). The rhema revelations given to contemporary prophetic voices can help guide us in the paths chosen by the Holy Spirit. Sometimes these "words" are partial revelations, and require other parts of the Body of Christ to help us determine the missing pieces of the puzzle. But, I have greatly benefited from prophetic words shared with me from numerous reliable prophetic individuals. By "reliable" I mean precise and accurate with rhema revelation.

There is a profound irony in being a prophetic individual. Not only do some receive "good" news for people, but some of us also receive apparently "bad" news for people. A prophet must maintain an attitude of optimism about God's sovereign over-arching principles as he or she delivers these latter "tough" words that are occasionally not welcomed. A prophet can have a rebuke, a caution, a warning, etc. Yet, he or she must present this tough word in a loving way that is most likely to produce a positive outcome by the recipient. The prophet seeks to produce hope in the listener, even if the news is not favorable. The purpose is to help draw the listener toward God's counsel (and without the messenger being an obstacle), although the listener can chose to reject the prophetic word or counsel.

One can know a great deal of information (i.e., *facts*) about an issue and yet be very deceived and lacking understanding of the *truth*. One might have a worldview or demonic influence that blocks the ability to interpret and understand. On the other hand, one might have very little information (few facts) about an issue and yet be enlightened to the truth. God chooses to confound the "wisdom of the wise" with the so-called "foolishness" of the simple. This paradox works in terms of living by the eyes of sight vs. the eyes of faith. This irony also works in terms of natural carnal knowledge vs. special revelation (e.g., a prophetic *word of knowledge* or a prophetic *word of wisdom*).

We must not rely <u>only</u> on carnal knowledge. By way of example, a scientist can know plenty of *facts* concerning biology and biochemisty. Yet, he or she can entirely miss the truth of God as the Creator of all things. Scripture indicates that it is foolishness to deny the presence of an Almighty God. By contrast a supernatural prophetic word of knowledge given in a dream or vision (often with strange symbolism written in a unique "language" of the Spirit) can be spoken to a stranger whom you have never met before, and this information can be pure truth with piercing effect. When a divine word of wisdom is shared with someone, it can provide an insight to solving a problem or puzzle. When Heaven invades earth, a paradigm is shifted from knowing mere facts to experiencing the truth. Facts alone can be used deceptively. It happens all the time in courts by prosecutors, defenders, and witnesses. But Jesus declared, "You shall know the Truth and the Truth shall set you free."

FALSE PROPHETS & FALSE TEACHERS

It is time that we hear more teaching on the topic of *false prophets and false teachers*. The Holy Spirit has impressed upon me warnings from Isaiah 30, Jeremiah 7, 20, 23, Amos 2, and I Kings 22, where the genuine prophets' *negative* words were intentionally suppressed. Look to the examples of these few prophets, who spoke warnings while the other so-called prophets, who greatly outnumbered them, were only tickling the ears of the hearers with "nice" words.

Innumerable false prophets and false teachers have inundated us in the Western world. Many local churches have been overrun by false teachers and false prophets, and some of them have the titles of "apostle, bishop, prophet, evangelist, pastor, or teacher". They are prone to *only* saying pleasant words that tickle the ears of the hearer with encouraging notions (2 Timothy 4:3-4). Thus, the *spirit of encouragement* is being usurped! False teachers and false prophets have laid claim to it, and have perverted it! Many of these false teachers are afraid to declare that repentance is the *only* on-ramp to salvation. Many are afraid to mention sin or to discipline those in sin. Many are afraid to declare the exclusive claims of Jesus. Many are afraid that if they do so, they will lose numbers of attendees or income from "their" congregation for their building fund. Many are afraid that people won't like them if they speak the truth. The root causes of this problem are the *fear of man* and the *desire to be liked*, which are fueled by pride.

Genuine prophetic voices must speak both pleasant and unpleasant truths. Prophetic individuals do bring encouragement, but that is not all that they bring. Evil King Ahab of Israel said of the righteous prophet Micaiah, *"I hate him because he never prophesies anything good about me, but always bad."* (I Kings 22:8). Ahab preferred the pleasant flattery and lies of 400 false prophets, rather than the tough words of Micaiah, who spoke only the truth coming from the Source of all divine truth. When asked to give the King some "nice" words, Micaiah replied, *"As surely as the Lord lives, I can tell him only what the Lord tells me."* (I Kings 22:14). Oh Lord Jesus, give us more Micaiah's of honor in our day! Father, give us prophetic men and women, who care more about Your agenda than their own agendas, regardless of the personal cost.

Failure by prophetic individuals to say tough words, cautions, warnings, corrections, and to perform the necessary disciplinary actions has resulted in a major departure from the *truth*. We need the *Whole Counsel of the Lord*. Many, if not most, of our leaders need a wake up call. Our society and church leaders are often more prone toward dishonesty than toward honesty. We're more prone to lawsuits and contortions of information. Honesty with full disclosure is the high road. But, it is harder to stay upon it, because it is a narrow path. I have a special wall hanging that includes a slogan resembling, *"Integrity is one of many paths, but it distinguishes itself from the rest by being the only one upon which you never get lost."*

Not only is the mouthpiece of the prophetic word held responsible, but so is the recipient of the word held responsible. Prophetic words that are *true* have two dimensions: (a) What was the actual precise word that was revealed for the benefit of the recipient? and (b) What did the recipient do with it? A prophetic word is often conditional on actions by the hearer.

To demonstrate the link between the giver of the "word" and the recipient, look at Jesus' teaching in Matthew 13 or Luke 8 concerning seeds. The rhema Word of God is like the seed being broadcast upon a plowed field. The soil (the recipient) determines the outcome of the seed's potential. The seed has the same high-level potential on either receptive life-giving soil or on the opposite, hard soil. The *potential* for fruit is determined by the seed (prophetic word), whereas the *outcome* is determined by the soil (recipient). If the recipient combines the seed with genuine faith, then it becomes a destiny-fulfilling fruit-bearing process. This initial action represents one step towards God's desired outcome. If faith is present from the beginning, then it is like a seed that just begins to germinate after being planted. However, if the recipient combines the rhema word with disbelief, doubt, and/or laziness, the intended full destiny is snuffed out. Therefore, a profound powerful rhema word can easily "fall short" of its stated goal, because the recipient didn't operate in *risk-taking belief in action* in agreement with that word. In the event that a word falls short over time, let us not be quick to point the finger at the prophetic mouthpiece, let us also consider the recipient's level of belief and action in response to the imparted word. Both seed and soil play critical roles.

When it does work as God intended, sometimes people will ask inquisitively, *"How did you know that?"* In all honesty, it just flows out of the indwelling Holy Spirit as a perceived, *"I know that I know"* assurance with some measure of certainty. The revelation can be either an internal "knowing" or a "graphical" prophetic revelation. The latter is more common in "seer" prophets, who routinely see images that provide symbolic clues to their prophetic understanding.

Note that the delivery and fulfillment of prophecy is tightly interwoven with faith. I commonly have a hard time recognizing the distinction between a rhema revelatory word from that of a faith declaration. Frequently they seem to blend together into one, just as a husband and wife blend together into one. Prophecy and faith appear to be ingredients of one another.

As one example of how the Lord uses a person, consider how the prophetic operates in my own life. There are many forms and manifestations of prophetic gifts and callings. I do not characterize the prophetic gift operating in my life as a "seer" calling *per se* (i.e., graphically-oriented while awake). I "see" by night in dreams and visions, but I "know" by day. This probably represents a typical or "common" prophet or prophetic person. Seers are less common. Daytime visions or trances occasionally happen in my life, but not routinely. When they happen (rarely) they are very important milestones or advance warnings to make me alert.

Dreams are common for me, and I probably dream every night. Typically I wake each morning and record multiple dreams in my journal. By God's grace and training it seems that He's progressively forming me into a more precise and accurate receiver and interpreter of dreams. This has been especially significant since 1997, when it began to accelerate as I stepped out in greater obedience to this prophetic calling. I made many mistakes and misinterpretations with dreams during this training phase. I haven't arrived yet, but I sense that I'm arriving at a higher level of reliability in interpretation. Each individual must learn to decipher the unique "language" of the Spirit that operates in his or her life. This is very important. One cannot merely read a book by some other prophetic author and learn all the keys to the unique "language" of the Spirit to that one particular individual. There are some aspects in common, but also some aspects that are unique to the individual. One must learn the process for himself or herself.

Actually the start of the flow of power of the Holy Spirit in my life was in 1987 while in London, England. It started with a sequence of three significant dreams all about spiritual warfare issues: (a) attempting to cast out a demon from a dog unsuccessfully; (b) discerning occult witches; and (c) preaching within a subterranean Hell to demonic hordes, just like Jesus likely did immediately prior to the Resurrection (1 Peter 3:18-20; Ephesians 4:7-10). The three dream messages in aggregate indicated that the Lord wanted to train me to cast out demons, to discern and confront witchcraft, and to be a prophetic preacher involved in spiritual warfare for the advancement of His Kingdom. This was an initial "calling" for me to recognize some of His purposes for my life. At that time I knew nothing about contemporary prophecy or prophets.

At risk of being considered crazy I told our local pastor in South Woodford in northeast London about these three dreams. They appeared to be very vivid and significant and were impressed upon my spirit. I knew I had to do something about these dreams, even if the pastor was to be skeptical about the value of dreams. It turned out to be a stimulus for me to begin itinerant preaching within our local congregation and other affiliates, which this pastor had been praying for concerning me. By sharing about the three dreams it was mutually encouraging. Then, the next spiritual dream was a precise message of caution for this pastor concerning a future event within our local congregation. I believe this latter dream changed history in advance. I "saw" the event happen in advance, and then later witnessed it take place precisely as per the dream, albeit with an altered favorable outcome. The dream was given as a stimulus to avert a potential problem.

All that to say, dreams and their interpretations are very important in my life and in many of my friends' lives. I teach on the important role of dreams in guiding people within the Bible as well as in contemporary life today. A search on this topic in the Scriptures surprises many people. For a notable example, one of the wisest decisions ever made by the wisest man who ever lived happened while he was *asleep*! Ironically very few people have ever noticed this fact. Often Bible teachers tell Solomon's story in error as if he made this decision (i.e., to ask for God's discernment and wisdom) consciously while awake. In addition, there are the multiple dreams and interpretations experienced by the two Josephs. One was the son of Jacob and the other was the non-biological father of Jesus. The use of dreams by God in Scripture is ubiquitous in the Old and New Testaments.

Today it is very common for God to use dreams to give guidance, warnings, and encouragement. But it takes training to begin to "master" this lost skill that many of us are just starting to re-learn in the Western Church. It is a valuable tool for the Kingdom of Heaven that the devil has sought to suppress using Greco-Roman rationalism and Western philosophy. One manifestation of the over-emphasis on rational understanding is Cessationism, which is a set of theological beliefs that have sought to deny the power of the Holy Spirit to move today in supernatural means, just as in the days of the writers of the Bible. Cessationists are particularly frightened by contemporary prophecy. I've seen it first hand. It freaks them out. Their fear is largely due to their lack of positive personal experiences coupled to a suppression or denial of the relevance of an overwhelming body of Scripture in support of the continuity of the supernatural power of the Holy Spirit.

The language of dreams is a spiritual language, that one must become trained to interpret. Many, if not most, dreams are highly symbolic in nature. Most dreams are not intended to be interpreted literally, although some are. Once a framework of dream interpretation is established in a trained individual, coupled with the present-tense guidance and discernment of the Holy Spirit, dream interpretation can be a very powerful tool. For instance, it can reveal warnings and can be very encouraging for the intended parties. Many of my prophetic friends and I have personally experienced this many times. We've witnessed God's revelation impact someone like a glass of iced tea with lemon quenching thirst on a hot August day in the desert sun. The dream's interpretation by someone skilled in this spiritual discipline can lift a heavy heart.

Listen for His *now* words for your own guidance. *"Whether you turn to the right or to the left, your ears will hear a voice behind you, saying 'This is the way; walk in it.'"* (Isaiah 30:21).

UNDERSTANDING OUR DAYS

I believe that we are in a serious season of *warnings*. This is not a season to only hear pleasant sugar coated partial truths. This is not a good time to *"command the prophets not to prophesy"* (Amos 3:12b). We are in serious times, especially for Israel, the USA, the United Kingdom, and Europe. For instance in January 2004, the Holy Spirit revealed to me that we had entered a season of the *"eye of the needle of the hurricane"*, which I declared publicly. Then starting later in 2004, we began to encounter the worst season of hurricanes in the recorded history of the Gulf of Mexico. We had passed out of the relative calm of the eye of the hurricane and into the destructive winds of its figurative backside.

Prior to then (ca. 2000-2003) my elderly prophet(ess) friend Mamie Jo Hunter spoke some important revelations to me immediately prior to her convalescence. Two are especially worth noting at this time: (a) *"A spirit of confusion has been released on the world"*; and (b) *"In the days ahead they will no longer follow the man with the black purse, they will follow the man with the black book!"* Money will not meet needs in the days of adversity. Folks will flock to those who know God's written Word (logos) and who hear the Holy Spirit's voice (rhema). *"The days are coming,' declares the Sovereign Lord, 'when I will send a famine through the land – not a famine of food or a thirst for water, but a famine of hearing the words of the Lord.'"* (Amos 8:11). My prophetic friends and I believe we are soon approaching those days. It wouldn't take much to produce a pandemic of anxiety, driving masses of people to those who have solid Biblical answers to the pressing questions of the day. You'll want to be someone who has a full supply of "oil" in your lamp in those days. If your lamp isn't full of precious Holy Spirit oil, what will you have to offer others who lack hope?

Many Christians today pray for the hastening of the *Day of the Lord*. Yet, I believe that the *Day of the Lord* will be a terrible day for *most* people. Read Nahum, Zephaniah, Amos, and Malachi. I appreciate what my friend Rob Learmonth in London once shared with me, *"Woe to you who long for the day of the Lord! Why do you long for the day of the Lord? That day will be darkness, not light. It will be as though a man fled from a lion only to meet a bear, as though he entered his house and rested his hand on the wall only to have a snake bite him. Will not the day of the Lord be darkness, not light; pitch-dark, without a ray of brightness?"* (Amos 5:18-20). Like the song from the comic movie of the 1980's Ghostbusters, *"Somethin's strange in the neighborhood...who ya gunna call?"* Who are you going to call in that day? Who can provide you with

God's counsel in that day of need? Who will provide you with words of hope in that day? Who ya gunna call?

Only those who understand the Scriptures like the *sons of Issachar*, who discerned well the times with rhema insight, will have the answers to the *spirit of confusion* and the *spirit of hopelessness*. These modern sons of Issachar will have discernment, will receive revelation, and will have their prayers answered. May your own personal oil jug be filled with the oil of hope prior to that day. May it never run dry during the season of testing.

Many precise and accurate prophetic individuals are hearing these "warnings" at present. What are you hearing? To whom are you listening? Who has influence in your life? Genuine prophetic individuals can give us advance warning and caution to get prepared for what is about to happen. Therefore, we don't need to be caught off guard. We don't need to be shocked when hardship arrives suddenly, like the destructive events of 9/11. Prophecy has a valuable role and purpose for the benefit of the entire Church (and world). However, some do not avail themselves of this important equipping role.

The pattern of prophetic "watching" is clearly portrayed in Ezekiel 3, 22, and 33. Prophetic individuals can be like watchmen on the tower surveying the horizon for any attacks by the enemy. Their job is to see this in advance, and to report it. God desires for us to be connected with genuine prophetic voices, who serve as watchmen on the tower.

I'll give you two examples concerning illnesses. In a dream or night vision I saw my natural father sitting in a chair in a hospital accompanied by my two sisters, Theresa and Maureen. He was there for diagnosis. As I stood nearby I declared to my father, *"You have had a minor stroke with partial paralysis affecting one side of your body"*. But, I knew that he would recover from this episode and be OK. I recorded it in my journal and prayed for God's purposes to be fulfilled. Then, one week later this precise event happened. Theresa wrote me an e-mail explaining that she and Maureen had been in the hospital with Dad. The details were the same. She asked for prayer for Dad. My reply was, *"I already saw this in a dream and recorded it in my journal a week ago. But, Dad will be OK."* It shocked my sister somewhat. It did in fact turn out as the dream/vision had indicated in advance.

A second example happened while being a guest speaker at Grace Covenant Church north of Chicago, care of the invitation of my friend Pastor Derek Kuhn. As I was walking down the aisle leaving the morning session, I spotted a woman. I approached this stranger and asked her, *"What is wrong with your eyesight, and in particular your left eye?"* She looked fine, and there was no evidence of any eyesight problem. She replied that she was a doctoral student in a local evangelical seminary and that her vision was becoming impaired. Furthermore, her mother recently had her left eye surgically removed. I explained to her that I had "seen" a woman closely resembling her in a dream the prior night. In the dream I saw "her" left eye was damaged like a cracked glass eyeball, yet sewn together with silver (metal) suture thread. I sensed that God desired to expose to the light a problem within her family affecting eyesight. That which holds power in the darkness can lose its power once it is exposed to the light. When this brief encounter was over she said to me that she was a bit fearful and knew that I would have a word to speak to her, even though we had never met before.

These are two of many examples of God providing advance notice of His plans and/or the plans of the enemy. I desire to know both… God's plans as well as the enemy's! Shouldn't we be prepared to know what is over the next hill? Shouldn't we be as prepared as possible to engage in effective spiritual warfare?

Some of you might be asking, *"How do I connect with reliable prophetic people?"* I suggest you ask your local ministers, who are "open" to the gift of prophecy, if they have any recommendations. If that approach is not successful or not even possible given your circumstances, then contact someone affiliated with one of the recognized prophetic ministries. Some selected prophetic ministries in the USA to consider include Kingdom Ministries International (Howard Morgan), Christian International (Bill Hamon), Glory of Zion (Chuck Pierce), and Morningstar Ministries (Rick Joyner). I have personally benefited from the apostolic-prophetic ministry and leadership in each of these groups, and that especially of Howard Morgan, with whom I am a good friend.

I do have a caution to note. There are far more people who think they are highly prophetic than there are verifiable solid prophetic ministers. So, just going up to anyone and asking if they are "prophetic" might not serve your needs well. In addition, many well-intentioned "young" prophetic individuals pass through a season of training over many years in which they make quite a few mistakes. Howard Morgan humorously refers to this as the "Frankenstein" stage of prophetic development and training. It is awkward but necessary, as the Spirit is moving upon these inexperienced prophetic folks. The inexperienced can have *signal-to-noise ratio* imbalances during the learning curve.

I passed through it by myself, in large part because I didn't have a lot of mentoring in this "new" gift of prophecy. At least I would like to think that I've largely passed through this "Frankenstein" phase of training! Much of what I learned by myself was through "new" spiritual experiences, and without a historical Pentecostal frame of reference that is often typical. I went through most of this "foreign" journey as an Evangelical without any prophet to come along side of me and to mentor me. I didn't even know any prophets by name, and had never conducted a Bible study on the supernatural gift of prophecy. The Holy Spirit took me on this rhema journey in spite of my heritage and local church affiliations, which were not especially friendly toward contemporary prophecy. I got to where I am by His Spirit's active will working in spite of what seemed beyond or opposed to the "norm" for that type of church environment (i.e., non-charismatic, non-Pentecostal, Evangelical), and coupled to obedience on my behalf. But, mentors can greatly facilitate the learning curve with this supernatural spiritual gift.

Prophetic voices help us sort out the chaos of life. They infuse us with hope during times of difficulty. But, not all words are perceived as "positive". Some are clearly "negative" words involving rebuke, counsel, warnings, or cautions. As examples of prophetic ministry including "negative" words, consider the following testimonies.

I would like to share with you some of my impressions of what is happening spiritually within the USA at the time of writing of this book (i.e., completed in mid-2007). I had the privilege of participating during the National Day of Prayer in intercession for our nation and certain governmental leaders on Capitol Hill in Washington, DC on May 5th, 2005. That interesting "coincidental" date was 5-5-5.

The Holy Spirit routinely reveals things to me in spiritual dreams/ nighttime visions. Often this occurs just prior to a ministry event, thus giving timely insight about that event or revealing hidden clues about what is going on behind the scenes. One of the nights prior to traveling to Washington DC, I had a symbolic spiritual dream with two scenes that I felt was relevant to what the Holy Spirit was saying about the USA at that juncture. On 5-5-5 I shared the following insight with others:

In this dream my "pet" was dead on the ground and its visceral organs were spilled out of the abdomen, similar to a road kill animal. "I" (or whomever I represented in the dream) heard a sizzling sound, resembling meat cooking in a frying pan on a stove. I looked down at the entrails and noticed some movement as multiple large parasites emerged from the intestines. They had grotesque hard chitinous exoskeleton shells and were segmented. Each crustacean-like parasite was approximately two inches long by one inch wide. They vaguely resembled dark brown ancient trilobites or "rolly polly" insects. I was told by the *Voice* to, *"Stick a fork in it!"* So, I jabbed through the entrails repeatedly in order to attempt to kill the ugly parasite creatures. When I was done jabbing with the fork, I picked up the carcass, but it immediately turned into a green corn husk that was hollow with no corn or cob inside. The grain, too, had been consumed from the inside by parasites. I shook it to make sure there was no corn inside. It was empty. Not one kernel of corn remained.

As I pondered the meaning of this symbolic dream, I sensed that the "pet" represented America. A pet represents something for which we're very fond and intimately aware. Yet, a pet isn't precisely at the same top level of importance as our personal "family". It is a notch below in relative importance to our lives. Our personal priorities should be *faith, family,* and *friends,* and finally other things, such as our nation. Unfortunately, this beloved pet (and ear of corn) had been consumed internally by parasites. America has very serious deep problems on its "insides".

Our nation and many of our leaders have largely forsaken Joshua 1:8, *"Do not let this book of the Law depart from your mouth; meditate on it day and night so that you may be careful to do everything written in it. Then, you will be prosperous and successful."* Because of this we are being eaten up from the inside by "demonic" forces of evil that we have granted permission to reside here. To *"stick a fork in it"* means two things: (a) to destroy the internal evil beings; and (b) *"it is finished"*. The transformation into an ear of corn is symbolic of God's intended "harvest" and provision of food and seed for the future. It was obvious that the internal damage destroyed the nation's future potential for God's intended "harvest" of souls and prosperity.

I interpret the serious implications as: (1) May we repent and pray that God Almighty be merciful to our nation and our nation's leadership at this juncture. We must kill off the internal evils that we have tolerated, for they are sucking the life out of us individually and our nation corporately. This is a serious and present warning. The pet had already died, and it was too late to resuscitate it when the fork was used against the parasites. This is a call to repentance by the people of the USA and our governmental and spiritual leadership. We must act now to seek His face and His favor; and (2) the pair of unrelated images of the pet and the corn provided internal *confirmation*, just as Joseph explained about the pair of unrelated images from Pharaoh's dreams provided *confirmation* of their intended meaning. The two symbols confirm a single reality. Ironically, the consumption of an animal (a pet) and an ear of corn has some similarity to Pharaoh's pair of dreams related to the consumption of animals (cattle) and heads of grain. Pharaoh's pair of dreams revealed a time of famine was soon to strike the land, and it in deed came to pass.

A confirmation of the pet/corn dream's message was also given to me via another dream or night vision. I have experienced dreams of meeting President George W. Bush and other foreign leaders about God's desires for nations. In the following dream/vision I was with President G.W. Bush. "I" was co-hosting with President Bush a group of military veterans inside the White House. It was a day of honoring them for their service, and I had arranged this meeting and had invited the guests. It was a pleasurable meeting with refreshments. Bush and I were "friends" talking with one another in this meeting. I asked him to honor our veteran guests by giving each one a small token memento from the White House to remember this significant day. He asked his staff to bring in a table with small gift items, such as coffee mugs and ink pens emblazoned with the White House insignia. I then told the military veteran guests they were each entitled to one small White House gift.

As I looked at the table I noticed a stack of approximately ten historic leather-bound journals. I asked President Bush, *"Who wrote them? Are these also gifts for us?"* He replied, *"These books were written by George Washington, and 'yes' you may take one of them as a gift".* These priceless books contained biographical insights written by President George Washington himself about the history of our nation's foundation. I looked at the bindings of the stack of books, and noticed the following with intrigue and alarm. The bottom book written by George Washington centuries ago was entitled "The Occult" and the third book from the bottom was entitled "Thyatira". These titles greatly discouraged me...like being punched in the gut. Even in the dream I knew what those book titles and order of books meant. They were not good books!

The veterans represent those deserving of honor for having fought for "us" in battles. This could be interpreted either literally as real military soldiers or symbolically as Judeo-Christian "soldiers" in spiritual warfare. The ten books represent the complete or full history of the founding of the nation according to George Washington in his own words during the 18th Century. Two parts of the ten were evil (~ 20 percent evil). The bottom book on "The Occult" was very disheartening to me, because it says that at our core our nation's foundation was tainted at the start by witchcraft and suggests that it was introduced at least in part via the hand of George Washington himself, for he "wrote" these volumes himself. *[This may be a hard word for many patriotic loyal followers of George Washington, whom many presume was a righteous Christian in good standing before the Lord.]*

THE CURSES OF FREEMASONRY

The significance of George Washington's writings within the dream or night vision relates in the natural world to two things: (a) George Washington's blatant embracing of Freemasonry, which is historically established as fact. Just go visit the display cabinet inside the lower level of the US Capitol Rotunda. He even laid one of the Capitol's cornerstones in a Masonic religious ritual; and (b) The *rebellion* against authority toward the throne in England, which at least in part was tainted with sin. Occult witchcraft is empowered by two stronghold forces — *rebellion* against the authority of others and *manipulation* to gain authority for oneself.

Freemasonry is one of many "on ramps" to the highway of the occult. It has appeal for unsuspecting and uninformed businessmen, who are seeking tangible benefits from joining. The recruits seek via joining the Masons to establish a sense of community and networking for business and social benefit. There is no doubt that the public persona of the Masons and their affiliated Shriners underscores their philanthropic good deeds, such as helping children or burn victims in trauma centers. However, the unsuspecting recruits are deceived by the organization's leadership, who know more about the religious nature of their oaths than the novice recruits. The consequences of agreement with the declared sequential curses as a Mason damage not only the man who joins this secret society, but also his family and their future. It produced binding curses on the family line, and from my perspective especially so the male lineage.

I have had some first-hand experiences in dealing with exposing this hidden evil imbedded in the descendants of Masons. It might be an eye-opener to some of you to learn about it. Satan does not want us to understand Freemasonry or the Shriners, for within the shrouded secrecy and declared curses there is some real power, albeit dark power of witchcraft. Many in the lower ranks of Freemasonry have yet to see the level of spiritual darkness of the "on ramp" to the occult. It is idolatry of a grievous form in the eyes of God Almighty. It is detestable and blasphemous to the true God of Abraham, Isaac, and Jacob.

With all of the recent attention drawn to the fictional *Da Vinci Code* and related media that has promoted interest in secret societies, I urge you to pay careful attention to what you choose to read and watch. This material is tainted with evil. If you or those you know are involved in Freemasonry or other secret society organizations, there is room for hope and personal redemption. Three actions are appropriate:

- RENOUNCE the secret society and its oaths and curses;
- REPENT of any involvement in the secret society; and
- REFOCUS your attention on the true God, Yahweh, instead of the cursed false gods.

In some instances, you might even need to have acts of deliverance performed by those trained in spiritual warfare to break the chokehold of the curses upon a family. This can involve deliverance from literal demons (i.e., exorcism). Scripture tells us that the sins of the fathers can visit the descendents up to the fourth generation. A seemingly "innocent" person, who is even a believer in Jesus, can be adversely affected by

---

the sins of a grandfather who was a Mason. I urge you, do not doubt the seriousness of this matter. Secret societies enslave their volunteer victims, who in turn voluntarily subject their spouses and descendents to enslaving curses. They choose to declare these harmful curses.

George Washington, the nation's founding President, was voluntarily involved in this occult movement. There have been at least 14 US Presidents to date, who have disclosed that they have been members of the Masons. There are many businessmen and government leaders today, who are involved in Freemasonry by choice. Not only do local church leaders fail to recognize the idolatrous evil of Freemasonry, but many even overtly condone the participation of church members in this occult organization. This is very common in the Deep South, and is not unfamiliar to many Bible-toting Southern Baptists in particular. It is one of the devil's strongholds over the Southeastern states. The devil uses a lot of tricks to enslave people, but this one is a deceptive and powerful delusion.

There should be no way possible for an informed righteous believer in Jesus to embrace and condone Freemasonry. Idolatrous and occult practices should not be tolerated by the true Church. The secret curses declared voluntarily by a Mason or a Shriner are idolatrous, giving honor to a false deity. Let us not forget that the highly revered President George Washington was an active participant in an overtly occultic organization. So, at America's founding, the nation and its people were already influenced by the curses of this organization...thus the foundational book's title was revealed within the dream as "The Occult".

Returning to the dream/vision, the third book from the bottom of the stack was entitled "Thyatira" reinforces the first book's meaning. Thyatira speaks of the church that tolerates the spirit of rebellion and manipulation, commonly referred to as "Jezebel". This says that America (or the "church" in America) was founded with this "Jezebel" as a parasitic component. Some of the characteristics of the "Jezebel" spirit are hard-driving, forceful, self-promoting, hyper-controlling, and manipulative. These characteristics are common in many Americans, both male and female. In the USA we routinely hold in high regard this "spirit" that is contrary to the Kingdom of God.

Rather, the Almighty desires that we learn to live in the Spirit, not in the flesh. We must learn to *"Reign from our rear and not our head!"* This means that real Judeo-Christian spiritual authority and power comes from the place of "rest and peace". Not from striving. Not from intellectual, theological, doctrinal, and denominational knowledge. Not from forcefully pushing one's agenda. Not from self-promotion. Not from building one's own empire. The place of rest is found in the throne room in Heaven where Jesus the Christ is *seated* at the right hand of Father God! He's not worried about anything, and He has *all* authority and power. Where one is seated determines what comes out of his or her mouth. An anxious, driven, hurried man or woman is not in the place of rest that equates with *being in the Spirit.* The Western "church" as we commonly know it, is often way off on this point.

The Lord has revealed to me that *reigning from our rear* is an effective strategy to defeat *witchcraft,* which at its roots has two principle components: (1) *rebellion* against the authority of others; and (2) *manipulation* to seek control and authority over others. They are two sides to the same coin. Those using witchcraft hate all forms of authority, unless it is their "own" authority to control others for their own agenda. These two linked characteristics are at the core of the devil's strategy to usurp the rightful place of the Almighty. Rebellion and manipulation are incompatible with humility and grace.

Ruling from the place of rest is a powerful tool that releases genuine Holy Spirit authority and power. Rest produces *influence* over others, yet with real freedom on behalf of those being influenced! The willing listeners volunteer to follow, rather than being pushed into action. It is the opposite of witchcraft. The enemies of the Kingdom of God do not like for you to know this truth!

A stone pitched obliquely with momentum across the surface of a *calm* stream of water will skip off of it onto the opposite bank. But, the same stone striking the surface of a *turbulent* stream will immediately be absorbed into the water! The uneasy water will accept the attack or the offense. If we are at rest, we can repel the enemy's attack without it affecting us. May the water of the Holy Spirit keep us in a calm place of rest. Our hope and victory is found in rest.

In the dream/vision the remaining ~ 80 percent of the books' titles was fine, but this ~ 20 percent (i.e. "The Occult" and "Thyatira") was very disturbing. It is my prayer that you will take to heart this warning and pray for breakthrough over our land as men and women are drawn to repentance.

These examples of dreams/visions demonstrate that a prophetic voice must share not only the "good" things, but also the "hard" things that they see as prophetic watchmen. These warnings and cautions are for the good of mankind. If a prophetic voice *only* speaks of pleasant "blessings", you can be assured that they are misleading people. They must provide both the good along with the warnings. As I read the Scriptures I've noted an abundance of "negative" prophetic words. Jeremiah and other prophets warn us to not listen to so-called "prophets" who only tickle our ears with pleasantries. At its surface level, there appears to be nothing wrong with hanging out with only "encouraging" people. But, if their words are *always* "positive" and *never* deal with correction, reproof, or warning, then watch out. If their *positive-all-the-time* words are not inspired by the Holy Spirit, then we don't need to listen to their "false hope" generators. Do you understand the irony of this point? We want to express words of hope, but they must be based upon God's rhema and logos words, rather than on presumption. Yes, we want positive people around us. However, if *all* we hear are positive words, then we won't be open to hearing God-given warnings, cautions, and course corrections. We must have both. We must have Holy Spirit-inspired "positive" and "negative" words.

Some folks lack hope because their hope was based upon something that was ill informed and not entirely true. If you have accurate and precise Holy Spirit information, then you are likely to place your hope on solid ground that will not shake.

FAULTY THEOLOGY BASED UPON HALF TRUTHS

If our theology is build upon errors, then our belief system can actually become the quicksand that sinks us during times of crisis when we need hope. If it is not anchored in the truth, then it will not be sufficient to answer our cries for understanding. In this case, we will not find hope during times of need. Not only will it give us misleading or false answers, but it can also contribute to hopelessness.

Theological *half truths* can be lies that deny the *Whole Counsel of the Lord*. Several theological *half truths* have become very common in our day. I'll briefly mention a few of them here. But, I won't belabor each of the points, as I intend to devote another book to this topic in greater depth:

(1) If we do not fully embrace *all* of the Scriptural attributes and virtues of the Trinitarian God, then we will be out of balance. Many folks today only want to see the "nice" attributes of God or the "nice" Red Letter words of Jesus in the New Testament. They only want to see His love, grace, and forgiveness. They choose to disregard large portions of Scripture presenting other attributes, virtues, and requirements that they find less than warm. He is the *God of Love*. But, He is also the **God of Adversity**. Those who deny this reality have built a house on the shifting sands of poor theology.

Many people simplistically think, *"God is a good god, and the devil is a bad devil"*, as if *all* adversity in life comes from the devil. Well, it does not! I certainly agree that God is *always* good, and no evil exists within Him. But, even in His absolute goodness He is still a God of justice, judgment, chastisement, reproof, and testing of the hearts of men. Many folks these days have all but discarded any notions of the latter aspects of God's character. He is both good and a God of Adversity at the same time…an apparent paradox with which He is quite comfortable, even if we are not. Whether by the active or the passive Hand of the Lord, these attributes of the Creator (i.e., regarding adversity) are noted ubiquitously within the Scriptures.

Spiritual maturity demands of us to expound the Scriptures with greater precision to develop a theology based upon the *Whole Counsel of the Lord*. We must go beyond merely wanting our ears to be tickled by pleasant words. We need a more illuminated view of the *God of Adversity* so that we will grow in the *fear of the Lord*.

(2) Some people become bitter and disappointed when they don't receive what they wanted. Some have placed their reliance on the "***name it and claim it***" approach, which is common among many Charismatics. Yet, it often does not yield the anticipated result. We must face it – disappointments and delays are tough realities of life. When these folks are let down, they can lose hope. It can be devastating. It can cause a detour for decades in a walk of faith, and all because their theology had an improper emphasis from the start.

(3) Suffering can be useful and productive in our lives to train and equip us for work in the Kingdom. *"Therefore, since we have been justified through faith, we have peace with God through our Lord Jesus Christ, through whom we have gained access by faith into this grace in which we now stand. And we rejoice in the <u>hope</u> of the glory of God. Not only so, but we also rejoice in our sufferings, because we know that suffering produces perseverance; perseverance, character; and character, <u>hope</u>. And <u>hope</u> does not disappoint us, because God has poured out his love into our hearts by the Holy Spirit, whom he has given us."* (Romans 5:1-5; emphasis added). Paul also wrote, *"I want to know Christ and the power of his resurrection and the fellowship of sharing in his sufferings…"* (Philippians 3:10); and *"So do not be ashamed to testify about our Lord, or ashamed of me his prisoner. But join with me in suffering for the gospel, by the power of God…"* (2 Timothy 1:8).

Suffering can result in the generation of hope in those who are yielded to the hand of the Master Potter, as he pounds upon His clay. That is highly ironic. Remember that – suffering can produce hope, if one processes the pain well! Yet, many today have no room in their theological closet for any suffering. They just go around spouting, *"I reject that negative word in Jesus name!"* It is as if they overlook the obvious – Jesus himself faced countless obstacles, criticisms, threats, and attacks. Jesus and Paul said that a true disciple should anticipate persecution and hardships (e.g., 1 Timothy 3:12). Hardships are the kilns that purify our character.

(4) Prosperity Theology is based upon a *half truth* that emphasizes God's desires to bless us abundantly. But, on the other side Prosperity Charlatans deny major portions of Scripture to feed their ravenous greedy appetites. This all-too-common practice must be exposed and confronted head on! It is greed and manipulation cloaked in the robes of a minister (see 1 Timothy 6:3-19).

Have you ever entered a "church building" and encountered:

- a series of collections taken one after another for various tithes and offerings in a single meeting?
- intentional pressures to produce guilt and shame about the financial "needs" of the local church, which often are really exaggerated "wants" going well beyond real "needs"?
- on the bookstore's shelves is a section on the theme of Finances,

in which many of the books focus on becoming a Christian millionaire?

- prominent displays of the pastor's image, name, books, and recordings, and perhaps portraying him living an affluent lifestyle?
- The ministry's website is coincidentally the name of the minister, rather than the name of the congregation or ministry?

What is wrong with this picture? What is wrong with us for participating in this? Are we spiritually asleep or what?

As the Batman TV series concluded each episode back in the 1960's, *"Stay tuned, same bat time, same bat channel!"* If these topics grab your attention, stay tuned as I intend to probe deeper on each of these issues in another book that has already begun. Until then, check the Path Clearer website for relevant information – www.pathclearer.com.

Brothers and sisters, we need precise and accurate prophetic voices coupled with the gift of discernment to know where correction is necessary today in the Body of Christ Jesus. Prophetic voices and discerners need to boldly speak out in order to expose the *half truths* that lead to lies. Oh Father, give them courage to stand up and speak out!

ONE LITTLE BIRDIE

Before leaving this important topic about the *gift of prophecy*, I have one final anecdote to share. I had a dream in which two bird nests contained small immature birds. They resembled baby swallows or swifts with black feathers. A large predatory bird of another species was pecking at them, so I grabbed the predatory bird with my hand and killed it to protect the young birds.

Upon waking I mentioned the dream to Laura, recorded it in my journal, and pondered its possible significance. I was attempting to interpret some spiritual meaning for the days ahead (e.g., perhaps about shepherding and protecting children or young immature disciples). A few hours later I was sitting at my desk and heard a noise inside of our closed fireplace. Inside of it was a small black-colored bird resembling a swallow or a swift. Excitedly I called Laura to help me catch it, once we opened the glass doors to the fireplace. We used a net to gently restrain it, and then took it outside. With hearts of gratitude we released it and enjoyed seeing it fly away. Had I not been there at my desk that particular morning the little bird probably would have died of dehydration, as it was just a small baby bird learning to fly.

Then, a few days later I was trimming the hedges in front of our home, and I almost inadvertently cut into a small bird nest with eggs concealed within the brush. Fortunately the nest and eggs were spared. As I experienced this second *Déjà vu* incidence, I looked overhead and there was the "mother" bird a few feet away resting on the edge of the gutter and watching me.

For many weeks I pondered why the Lord had shown me a dream just so that I would be prepared to release this little bird from our fireplace and to protect some eggs. What did it mean? Then, some time later while driving my car a profound *inner knowing* prompting of the Spirit suddenly hit me and immediately brought me to tears. The Lord revealed to me to not over-spiritualize or over-interpret what had happened in the dream and the events that followed shortly thereafter. It was as if I "heard" Him impress upon my spirit the following simple words, *"I did it because I care for that little bird!"* Along with this simple revelation was an immediate confirmation of His deep love for us in the words of Jesus, *"Are not two sparrows sold for a penny? Yet not one of them will fall to the ground apart from the will of your Father. And even the very hairs of your head are all numbered. So don't be afraid; you are worth more than many sparrows."* (Matthew 10:29-31).

6

TURN YOUR WEEPING INTO LAUGHTER

For his anger lasts only a moment, but his favor lasts a lifetime;
weeping may remain for a night, but rejoicing
comes in the morning.

~ Psalm 30:5

Life throws many difficulties into our paths. Of these, perhaps two of the greatest obstacles to overcome are loneliness and the deaths of loved ones, and especially the untimely deaths of the young. My family has experienced the tragic deaths of several young relatives, including my brother Pat, my brother Dan's newborn son Corey, and my first cousin Susan. I've also performed CPR on a 14-year old victim of drowning, after my good friend John Manwell retrieved the boy's body from the bottom of a lake. However, I was unable to restore life to the boy in spite of CPR and fervent prayer.

"Even though I walk through the valley of the shadow of death, I will fear no evil, for you are with me; your rod and your staff, they comfort me." (Psalm 23:4). Even in these times, He is with us. In these times He desires to exchange our ashes for His beauty. But, it is nonetheless emotionally painful.

If you have any measure of compassion whatsoever, you wouldn't wish loneliness upon your worst enemy. It can be devastating. Loneliness is a condition of the heart that can drain all of the life force out of one's countenance. Loneliness is like a hope-sucking vacuum. In the mid-20th century, Patsy Cline's swooning song of romantic desire, *"Walking After Midnight"*, captures well the sentiment of loneliness:

I go out walking after midnight
Out in the moonlight just like we used to do
I'm always walking after midnight searching for you

I walk for miles along the highway
Well that's just my way of saying I love you
I'm always walking after midnight searching for you

I stopped to see a weeping willow
Crying on his pillow maybe he's crying for me
And as the skies turn gloomy
Night blooms will whisper to me I'm lonesome as I can be

I go out walking after midnight out in the moonlight
Just hoping maybe you're somewhere walking after midnight searching for me

I have noted during prayer times at ministry events that there are plenty of lonely people. They come in all types; single, married, divorced, and widowed. Whether they never "had" or formerly "had" and then "lost" a key relationship, it matters little. What matters is their "present" state of perceived need or desire. This is especially true of women. They are designed by the hand of God to be in tune with their emotional need to give and receive nurturing. Some men barely perceive this concept, but most women are hard-wired with a deep primal and spiritual need to be loved and to love. My own precious wife, Laura, is a fine example of a nurturer. I am so grateful to God for her as my wife and as the mother to our four children. She is always concerned for her husband and children, and is willing to give selflessly.

Women are fulfilled largely through dialog and nurture! While men seem more concerned with solving problems and moving on to the next obstacle, women place a higher priority on communication. And, communication is at the core of nurturing. Psychologists comment about the typical woman's need for verbal communication exceeding that of men, although the number of words spoken daily when comparing men and women remains a topic of debate. Jesus said, *"But I tell you that men will have to give account on the day of judgment for every careless word they have spoken."*

—
82

(Matthew 12:36; emphasis added). Since He said "men", I guess that leaves the chatty women off the hook. [Just joking.]

Someone does not need to be *alone* in order to be *lonely*. Ironically the feeling of loneliness often manifests while in the midst of a huge crowd. It can happen while eating in a full restaurant by oneself on a business trip. Been there, done that countless times. Having enjoyed the privilege of traveling around the globe for the past two decades, I've visited many of the world's most populist cities, such as Chongqing (Chong King) in China, a multi-city metro area with 33 million people. I've also visited Bombay, London, New York, Tokyo, Seoul, Sydney, Los Angeles, among others. There is certainly no lack of people to meet along the journey and to establish a dialog if you're so inclined. Yet, at times being in these huge over-populated cities produces a profound melancholy. I feel so *insignificant* and lonely while walking the streets as cars drive past and other pedestrians seem entirely unaware of my presence. In a sea of humanity, we often feel even sub-human. We seem more like a mere insect in a vast jungle or a grain of sand on the ocean's shoreline. Being in these densely populated cities can produce a mental "funk" that saps vitality. I feel like if I fainted or died on the sidewalk, literally no one would even care to interrupt his or her busy-ness to stop and take note. Oh God, what is man that You are mindful of him?

Reinforcing this point, during the late 80's I was walking on a side-walk in London during the winter. I was on a quick-paced stroll from my workplace on Lincoln's Inn Fields toward the British Museum, my favorite site in all of London. It is full of invaluable objects chronicling Biblical history. While briskly walking, a Catholic nun and I discovered a dead man sitting slumped over in a doorway facing the street. Judging by his appearance and the white bottle of Malibu liquor resting next to his cold breathless body, he was a homeless alcoholic. We checked for signs of life and found none. Had we found any, she and I would have attempted to resuscitate or sustain this homeless man's life. But, finding none we arranged for an ambulance to remove the body.

Ironically, the place where this man died while all alone was *Bury Lane* in the West End of London, a metropolitan community of perhaps ten million people. This poignant example drove home that this man was so lonely that he didn't even have a single friend there to notice the time of his passing into the next realm. In a city of millions, perhaps loneliness precipitated his unfortunate condition. Even the writer of Proverbs notes that strong alcoholic drink is the elixir for those who are perishing…those without hope. Hundreds of millions of people each day take alcohol or drugs to attempt to receive temporary relief from their mental anguish, while loneliness is one of the major root causes of their persistent pain. In this context, I think of Hank Williams who crooned *"I'm So Lonesome I Could Cry"*:

> *Hear the lonesome whiperwill*
> *He sounds too blue to fly*
> *The midnight train is whining low*
> *I'm so lonesome I could cry*

> *I've never seen a night so long*
> *When time goes crawling by*
> *The moon just went behind a cloud*
> *To hide its face and cry*

> *Did you ever see a robin weep*
> *When leaves begin to die*
> *That means he's lost the will to live*
> *I'm so lonesome I could cry*

> *The silence of a falling star*
> *Lights up a purple sky*
> *And as I wonder where you are*
> *I'm so lonesome I could cry*

At its core loneliness robs oneself from the sense of belonging, of security, of trust, of having a meaningful existence. Humans want to be appreciated and needed by others. Unless you suffer from autism or a psychosocial disorder, don't you want to be shown affection and respect? The spirit of loneliness not only rehearses the losses of the past, moaning the current status of need, but it also reaches forward to strangle all hope of ever being in relationship with the individuals we desire to love us. The spirit of loneliness has the ability to permeate all other thoughts. It seems to take over the "priority-establishing mechanism" of the mind. It can dry up all optimism and can result in serious depression.

Another problem with acute loneliness is that the sufferer tends to either withdraw socially as a "loner" or tends to "smother" any tiny candle flame of an emerging relationship. The latter place unrealistic demands upon others to feed his or her need for relationship. Those prone to "smothering" can turn off other well-balanced individuals.

So, what do we do to confront the spirit of loneliness? Thankfully our God is a *relational* Creator. He didn't merely write a book and then go away as a good deistic god. He is alive! He wants us to be in relationship with Him. He is crying out for our attention. The eyes of the Lord move to and fro, searching for those who will passionately pursue a relationship with Him. He wants us to be in love with His son, Jesus, who knows well what it is like to be human. *"The Lord is good, a refuge in times of trouble. He cares for those who trust in him…"* (Nahum 1:7). Jesus came as a man on earth, so that He can relate with our frailties and needs. I don't fully understand His coming to earth as the Messiah Jesus, but it is the truth. Loneliness can serve as a stimulus to drive us to give more attention to our relationship with the Lord.

THE MANIFESTATIONS OF HOPE

Hope can be perceived differently by each of us. It is context dependent. The context is the framework of various challenges that test whether hope is present or not. Therefore, hope has many manifestations. Ponder the diversity of examples listed below that serve as evidences of the presence of hope:

- "Resting" while in the midst of crisis
- A cool drink of water provided to a parched laborer
- Imagining your children's future with joy
- Justice is served following a season of injustice
- Pardon and forgiveness for an offense
- Reward for a job well done
- Eternity spent with Jesus

- Anticipating an abundant harvest
- Discovery of a treacherous plot in advance
- A solid foundation upon which to build
- Sufficient supply for the needs of the day
- Glee in the eyes of someone healed or set free from sin's captivity
- Watching your son or daughter graduate or get married
- A pleasant night's sleep
- A well-fed child in a famine-afflicted land
- No more disease, no more pain, and no more tears
- Anticipation of answered prayer
- Laughing when you would rather cry
- Sleeping in the bottom of the boat during the storm

Let us learn to declare: Tomorrow is a new day! This, too, shall pass! Beyond every valley is another hilltop! And, after winter, spring brings refreshing sunshine! Our words can shift our mindset out of the gutter.

In a dream I was operating a vehicle on top of a bridge elevated hundreds of yards above the water. I couldn't see the bridge directly under me, but I could experience its effect. Yet, as I drove from the level spot at the top, it had a pitch so steep that I couldn't see the bridge ahead from my vantage point over the front of the vehicle. I had to "inch" forward in trust. What my eyes experienced was a car seemingly floating on air suspended a quarter of a mile over a lake. Slowly the car tipped downward to match the slope of the bridge supporting it. When I finally made it to the horizontal water level, then ahead of me I could see another bridge just prior to the entry of the city. This bridge was constructed of old beautiful stonework, but was also very steep up and down, like a volcano. However, having passed the first test that was scary because I couldn't see it, I could see the entire structure of the next bridge ahead of me well in advance. The "next" experience would be a bit easier, as I could trust what I had seen in advance.

We "learn" faith from our prior experiences, and once learned we have a spiritual framework in which to process in order to progress in faith during the next event. We learn that He is faithful and that He's a light and a lamp to our path.

JOE DOOLEY

One of the advantages of real hope is that it stirs up *prayers of faith* within us. My Uncle Joe Dooley suffered from a neurological problem that caused him to loose the ability to speak as he neared retirement age. He had been a loving husband and father, as well as a successful farmer on the land just west of my parent's farm. I really liked him. Whenever I traveled home to Kansas I enjoyed seeing him. At times my Dad and I would take Joe with us for a cup of coffee together at Drimmel's service station, the *do-drop-in* for locals in search of a coffee or a chilly beer or the latest gossip.

Joe had a tender heart, perhaps due to the loss of his only son as a child. I was one of Joe's nephews and he was kind to me. I was a close friend to his youngest daughter, Jeannie. For a season of life up to our early teen years, she was my best friend while living on adjacent farms. I had the privilege of working some on her Dad's farm for money.

During my teenage years I once messed up "big time" while driving Uncle Joe's big International Harvester tractor with a mounted cultivator. I was refueling it, which was quite a challenge because the tank's hose wasn't long enough to reach the tractor's tank. To get up close I carefully drove forward and straddled the support leg of the gravity-fed fuel tank between the tractor's tire and frame. I set the parking brake. But, unexpectedly the tractor rolled slightly when I released the foot brakes hitting the metal leg of this large full diesel tank, causing it to fall about ten feet to the ground. The hose broke off and it sprayed perhaps a hundred gallons of diesel all over the place. So, I jumped off the tractor's seat, and acted like a little Dutch boy sticking my finger in the hole to hold back the inevitable flood. I had diesel all over me from the tip of nose to my toes. But, that wasn't the worst part of the saga. Uncle Joe had warned me in advance about this perilous maneuver. Perhaps he, too, was a bit prophetic!

The underlying pathology of Joe's neurological problem was not clear, but the day-to-day manifestation certainly was, and it tried to rob his wife, Sara, and family of any hope of rebound to health. In the midst of this disheartening phase of chronic illness, I received many dreams about him that gave me hope that he could be healed by God from this affliction.

—

So, I prayed. And I prayed. Every time I managed to get back to Kansas for a visit I would go see Joe, then lay my hands on his head, and pray for a miraculous healing in this hopeless situation. But, the healing never came. However, I never gave up hope that God was more than able to do it. I continued this practice of praying for Joe for the remaining years of his life. Sometimes I went with my Dad or another companion; often times I went alone. The final five or so years of Joe's life were very difficult for his loyal wife, Sara, and his family. But, I did whatever I could. And, that was to believe and pray for a better outcome.

I don't know what effect my prayers might have had directly upon him. But, I am convinced of three things: (a) God was able to heal him; (b) God was testing my faith to obey His promptings via multiple dreams that portrayed hope within this hopeless situation; and (c) Those prayers demonstrated the *Heart of the Father* toward the family, who were processing their own pain and disappointment over losing the head of their household. The outcome of our prayers is God's business. We don't always receive what we desire. We just need to show trust and be obedient to the Spirit's promptings.

Eventually when Uncle Joe died I received a great honor in being asked to read the Scriptures and lead prayer at his funeral at St. Louis Catholic Church, several miles northwest from our family farms. It was a memorable and special occasion that really blessed me. I remain grateful to this day for being able to honor my uncle in that fitting manner.

EXCHANGING SORROW FOR DANCING

While in Europe in 2005 and 2006 our Path Clearer teams occasionally danced in the streets. One time was especially poignant. I was rapping an improvised song entitled *"Baruch HaShem"* (i.e., *Blessed be the Name* in Hebrew) in the Warsaw Ghetto district. This was the site of the infamous "Uprising" that resulted in many deaths. It is a gloomy somber place with the pallor of death. Our joyful dancing brought rays of "light" into those streets lined by apartment dwellings. Locals came up to us to learn why we were dancing and singing and clapping. To our pleasant surprise, a large tour group of Israeli Jewish youth arrived at the monument at that precise moment. They spontaneously joined us in the Hebrew rapping song and dance. They, too, were singing *"Baruch HaShem Adonai"*. It was entirely unexpected for both parties…a divinely arranged meeting to bring hope into a hopeless setting, and to give encouragement to the Israeli youth that Christians from the USA and UK were sympathetic toward them. They received joy when they had anticipated sober reflection.

Likewise, Jesus is delighted whenever we are torchbearers of light before the lonely, the downcast, and the hopeless. We can be the answer to their needs and prayers. We can help turn their sorrow into dancing and their weeping into laughter.

IT ISN'T ALWAYS AS MISERABLE AS IT SEEMS

The plans of the Sovereign Lord are vastly greater in span than our own limited experience. Olaudah Equiano was a Nigerian captured as a youth and taken into slavery in West Africa, the West Indies, and North America during the 18th Century. His biography tells of many fascinating stories of adventure. He wrote a wonderfully encouraging story concerning one trip while sailing from Cadiz, Spain toward England:

> *"When we were about the north latitude 42, we had contrary winds for several days, and the ship did not make in that time above six or seven miles straight course. This made the captain exceedingly fretful and peevish; and I was very sorry to hear God's most holy name often blasphemed by him. One day, as he was in that impious mood, a young gentleman on board, who was a passenger, reproved him, and said, he acted wrong, for we ought to be thankful to God for all things, as we were not in want of any thing on board; and though the wind was contrary for us, yet it was fair for some others, who perhaps stood in more need of it than we. I immediately seconded this young gentleman with some boldness, and said we had not the least cause to murmur, for the Lord was better to us than we deserved, and that he had done all things well. I expected that the captain would be very angry with me for speaking, but he replied not a word. However, before that time, or hour, on the following day, being the 21st of June, much to our great joy and astonishment, we saw the providential hand of our benign Creator, whose ways with his blind creatures are past finding out. The preceding night I dreamed that I saw a boat immediately off the starboard main shrouds; and exactly at half*

past one o'clock the following day at noon, while I was below, just as we had dined in the cabin, the man at the helm cried out, A boat! Which brought my dream that instant into my mind. I was the first man that jumped on the deck; and looking from the shrouds onward, according to my dream, I descried a little boat at some distance; but, as the waves were high, it was as much as we could do sometimes to discern her; we, however, stopped the ship's way, and the boat which was extremely small, came alongside with eleven miserable men, whom we took on board immediately. To all human appearance, these people must have perished in the course of an hour, or less; the boat being small, it barely contained them. When we took them up they were half drowned, and had no victuals, compass, water, or any other necessary whatsoever, and had only one bit of an oar to stir with, and that right before the wind; so that they were obliged to trust entirely to the mercy of the waves. As soon as we got them all on board, they bowed themselves on their knees, and, with hands and voices lifted up to heaven, thanked God for their deliverance; and I trust that my prayers were not wanting amongst them at the same time. This mercy of the Lord quite melted me, and I recollected his words, which I saw thus verified, in the 107th Psalm, 'O give thanks unto the Lord for he is good, for his mercy endureth forever. Hungry and thirsty, their souls fainted in them. They cried unto the Lord in their trouble, and he delivered them out of their distresses. And he led them forth by the right way, that they might go to a city of habitation. O that men would praise the Lord for his goodness, and for his wonderful works to the children of men. For he satisfieth the longing soul, and filleth the hungry soul with goodness…They that go down to the sea in ships; that do business in great waters; these see the works of the Lord, and his wonders in the deep. Whoso is wise and will observe these things, even they shall understand the loving kindness of the Lord.' The poor distressed captain said, 'that the Lord is good; for, seeing that I am not fit to die, he therefore gave me a space of time to repent.' I was very glad to hear this expression, and took an opportunity, when convenient, of talking to him on the providence of God. They told us they were Portuguese, and were in a brig loaded with corn, which shifted that morning at five o'clock, owing to which the vessel sunk that instant with two of the crew; and how these eleven got into the boat (which was lashed to the deck) not one of them could tell. We provided them with every necessary, and brought them all safe to London: and I hope the Lord gave them repentance unto eternal life." [The

—

Interesting Narrative and Other Writings by Olaudah Equiano (Edited by Vincent Carretta), Published by Penguin Group, 2003, pp. 200-202.]

This testimony of the high seas in 1775 provides us with several interesting anecdotes. First, from our limited understanding we might be in what seems to be distress or hopelessness, yet it is in fact the precise place that God wants us for His purposes to be accomplished. Had the winds been more favorable toward Olaudah's ship, it might not have been used as the providential "hand of God" to save the eleven men. Our personal discomfort might serve a greater good to be a blessing for someone else. Second, the young gentleman and Olaudah were of the right frame of mind to recall the Biblical admonition to "give thanks in all things". Rather than agreeing with the captain's sentiments of frustration (which was reasonable), these two stood on the higher ground to see with the eyes of faith. One tangible benefit of faith-in-love is that it takes us beyond very limited selfish selves into a realm where we begin to grasp a hint of his Sovereignty. And, third, the Lord chose to give revelation in a dream to Olaudah (which coincidentally was common and reliable in his life), in order to prepare him for the events of the following day, so as to be alert for a boat coming nearby in the vast open seas.

In the prior year onboard a ship traveling in the opposite direction, London to Cadiz, the former West African slave who became a Freeman, Olaudah Equiano repented on October the sixth, and had a supernatural and revelatory conversion experience. His actions of being "born again" happened upon a seafaring ship. Ironically, the ship's name was none other than "Hope"!

7
COULD BE WORSE

Later Jesus found him at the temple and said to him, "...stop
sinning or something worse may happen to you."

~ John 5:14

Which one of the books of the Bible is the most depressing? Although Ecclesiastes runs a close second, in my opinion there is no equal to the book of Job. Most of it is a bummer. In this depressing book, Satan approached God and asked to inflict difficulties against Job to prove to God that the only reason Job gave God honor was because God was especially good to Job. Satan accused that if Job's life *went to hell* (symbolically) that Job would surrender all notions of affection for the Creator. So, God granted this series of horrible tests by Satan to plague Job with a tornado that destroyed property and claimed the lives of his children. Then, he sent a horrible blistering skin disease on Job, resembling bullous pemphigous or infected boils.

Then, Satan tempted Job's wife. She succumbed to the overwhelming stress of it all. She was fed up at Job's piety and she blamed God for their afflictions. *"His wife said to him, 'Are you still holding on to your integrity? Curse God and die!' He replied, 'You are talking like a foolish woman. Shall we accept good from God, and not trouble?' In all this, Job did not sin in what he said."* (Job 2:0-10).

When Laura and I were raising our four young children, we often read books to them while sitting in our favorite rocking chair. I've always had an affinity toward rocking chairs, having broken or worn out perhaps half a dozen of them in my lifetime. There were plenty of memorable children's books from which to choose, but I had a fondness for <u>Could be</u> <u>Worse</u> by James Stevenson. This comical story unfolds as a sequence of exaggerated tales of woe. Each time the reader thinks the characters in the plot have run out of all hope, the narrator mentions, *"Well, it could be worse!"* At this pivotal intersection, he then proceeds to tell an even darker scenario. It's a funny book, meant to encourage and lift one's hopes to never give up, but to press on.

Even Jesus said to the lame man who had been healed after 38 years, *"Stop sinning or <u>something worse may happen</u> to you."* (John 5:14b; emphasis added). Our decisions to embrace sin can in fact invite harm upon our lives. So, when we think it can't get any worse, note that Jesus said that it could. Our actions determine in part what happens to us. Willful disobedience to the truth opens doors to the devil's influence. Things can get worse, for instance when God's mercy and protection are lifted from us when we walk in unrighteousness.

As a result of successfully leading the United Kingdom during one of its darkest periods in history in 1941 in World War II Winston Churchill quipped the now famous lines: *"Never give in. Never give in. Never, never, never, never—in nothing, great or small, large or petty—never give in, except to convictions of honor and good sense. Never yield to force. Never yield to the apparently overwhelming might of the enemy."* Churchill was once described by a close associate as one whose weaknesses were evident upon first encounter, however it would take a lifetime to appreciate his strengths.

PARALYSIS

Dennis Arnold has one of the most striking testimonies of any man. He exemplified persistence in spite of hardship. He was born into a poor family in Mississippi and his father was prone to drunkenness and belligerence. When Dennis was a young boy he developed polio and succumbed to paralysis of his legs. While he was hospitalized in Wisconsin at the age of seven he was placed inside of a body cast. There was no reason to be optimistic about the future. Paralysis, poverty, and a dysfunctional family were producing a hopeless scenario for this young boy.

Dennis was taken from the hospital by his parents to their "apartment", which was nothing more than a cold janitor's closet. They had little provision and the young boy became irritated and frustrated by his conditions. Just when you think it couldn't get any worse, it did. His father was also frustrated and could not accept that his son was a hopeless cripple with little potential to become a "real man". So, in rage he took a knife and removed the body cast from Dennis's small immobile body. He stood over Dennis threateningly and declared to the naked boy on the floor, *"I'm leaving you son. When I come back you better be either changed or dead!"* The father knocked out Dennis' mother with a punch, and left with the sound of the door locking in Dennis' ear. He lay on the cold cement floor naked and in the dark for several days and nights. His cries for help from inside the janitor's closet were not heeded by anyone.

But, when all hope was lost, a few days later a strange miraculous "presence" entered the locked janitor's room without opening the door. This "visitor" lifted the boy up and hugged him with warmth. The "visitor" sat him upon a chair and placed a sandwich in one hand and a glass of milk in the other. *[One might be prone to say, "That's almost unbelievable!" Yes, it is amazing. But, I personally know Dennis Arnold.]* As Dennis sat there on the chair, he heard the lock open and his parents entered the small room to their dismay as they witnessed this shocking scene of the boy sitting in the chair. Not only was Dennis visited miraculously, but he was also healed from polio. He could feel sensations in his legs and asked his father to help him take some steps, which he did.

Within the next year Dennis Arnold subsequently attended a church meeting and re-experienced the warmth and love of the strange presence from the "visitor". He then understood Who had visited him in that depressing cold janitor's closet in Wisconsin. He knew it to be the tangible love of Jesus. Dennis accepted Jesus as his Savior that day. And true to his miraculous testimony of healing, he persisted to believe in his healing and destiny ever since. This once immobile polio-afflicted boy was healed by the power of the Holy Spirit. Dennis subsequently went on to become an outstanding athlete in high school and a Gospel singer-songwriter with an excellent voice.

Dennis and I were introduced via a divine "coincidence", while each of us was obeying our own revelatory promptings of the Holy Spirit in January 2000 (see Praying Faith). When it seems like life can't get any more depressing and it could barely get any worse, there is always room for hope. Even at life's darkest moments, a tiny candle can begin to illuminate the darkness. Dennis' life is an example of God's gracious merciful touch to redeem something that appears to be worthless. Dennis Arnold is a living testimony of the power of a mighty creative and healing God!

Dennis continues to see the power of the Holy Spirit move miraculously and prophetically, and he breathes hope into the next generation. He would tell you in full agreement with the famous words of the great orator Winston Churchill, *"Never give in!"* It is never too deep or too dark for the miraculous power of God to reach into a situation and to turn it around to the glory of God. We must persevere in order to realize the desired outcome.

To top this story, not only do I know one formerly paralyzed individual who was healed miraculously. I know <u>three</u> of them as personal friends! Dennis Arnold (AL), Mamie Jo Hunter (GA), and Samuel Sorinmade (MA) were all healed of paralysis. Our God is still in the divine healing business today! In addition, once while at the Redemption Camp in Nigeria I watched with amazement the faith healing of a crippled man, who rose up from his mat and began to walk unaided like a spinning top. I know enough about physics to realize that this person's center of gravity required him to fall to the ground, yet the man stood upright as if suspended by a marionette string. It defied physical laws.

HOMELESSNESS

If you can afford to purchase a copy of this book there is a good probability that you at least have enough money to rent or own a place to stay. Among the most hopeless people are the homeless. Roger Miller epitomized the life of a carefree homeless vagrant in his song, *King of the Road*:

> *[Chorus] Trailer for sale or rent*
> *Rooms to let...fifty cents*
> *No phone, no pool, no pets*
> *I ain't got no cigarettes*
> *Ah, but..two hours of pushin' broom*
> *Buys an eight by twelve four-bit room*

I'm a man of means by no means
King of the road.

Third boxcar, midnight train
Destination...Bangor, Maine
Old worn out clothes and shoes,
I don't pay no union dues
I smoke old stogies I have found
Short, but not too big around
I'm a man of means by no means
King of the road.

I know every engineer on every train
All of their children, and all of their names
And every handout in every town
And every lock that ain't locked
When no one's around.

The homeless face extreme difficulties that most of us have never even contemplated for a second. I have had conversations with many homeless men over the past decade, and have sought to learn from them and their tragic lives. I've attempted to see the world from their hopeless perspectives. I could do something for them that they couldn't accomplish themselves. I could be a "voice" sharing their concerns.

Would you like to know some of the "tips" I've received from interviewing many homeless men? Not only are there the routine daily issues of seeking a meal and a safe place to sleep, but they often are the victims of other homeless thieves. That is why they often choose to sleep alone in horrible and frigid conditions, so as to not be hassled by fellow homeless men or women, who would take something from them given the chance. What little they possess during the day cannot be taken for granted. It might be taken from them at night while they sleep. They have no place to secure their possessions…not even a small footlocker.

The homeless know well that no more than ten percent of the "well off" in society will ever lift a finger to help them with a ride, a cup of hot coffee, or an apple. They can tell the difference between a genuine disciple and a pretend "Christian" from a mile away. Many will tell you this. They become proficient at discerning who will be the one who will help them while the nine walk away without making any eye contact. They are often more intelligent than most of us would give them credit.

When they lose their wallets, they lose their identity papers. Without an ID card, they can't be trusted by any governmental agency, business, or shelter. So, they become stuck in a no-man's land. Without an ID, they can't collect or cash checks. They can't open a postal mailbox or sign a contract or rent anything. No one will vouch for them. If you have ever been caught in a beaurocratic conundrum, this one takes the prize. They can be taken to jail and court, and they can't easily prove their own identity. They can be falsely accused of a crime, locked up for several days, and no one would want to advocate their case. Proverbs says that many are the friends of the wealthy, but few are the friends of the poor man.

They can't walk along a roadside or highway without the local police stopping to question or harass them. They are asked by the police to see their ID. If they fail the test, they are taken back to jail or escorted to some inconvenient location away from the local business district. They can't afford a bus ticket and they can't walk along the Interstate highway, so they can't leave town. They are trapped within a "Catch 22" with no car, no bike, no bus ticket, and no pedestrians are allowed to walk freely (that is if you look like a homeless person).

Our Scriptures are filled with examples where the righteous are admonished to make provision for the homeless and wanderer in the land (e.g., Isaiah 58). Yet, our culture and laws do not often honor these Biblical mandates. We are failing at this Kingdom activity, myself included.

While they are on the streets they encounter all sorts of unsavory fellows, the insanity of schizophrenics, the hostility of belligerent drug and alcohol addicts, the diseases of "cheap" prostitutes, the demon possessed, and to top it off the spite and indifference of the "well off", who have so much going for them. I've met some of these risky characters, and trust me you wouldn't want to let them sleep on your sofa at night. Yet, in the midst of such depressing situations, I have found some delightful and warm human beings. I've enjoyed hearing their stories. Many of them are veterans of foreign wars (e.g., Vietnam) and domestic wars (e.g., parents separated from their children). Many have served time in jail or prison, and some still carry weapons for protection. Many of them have knowledge of the Savior. Many of them genuinely want a way out of their pit. They just don't know how to break free from their hopelessness.

I do believe that there is one thing for us outside of this homeless scenario to realize – *we* can be the answer to their prayers. That's you and me. We, the royal plural, can help. The answer to their hopelessness can be found in our generosity and willingness to help. But, it takes courage to help. Sure, there are unsavory folks in their midst and one must act with wisdom. But, not all of the homeless are con men or beyond rescue. We can help them with clothing, meals, housing, and assistance in obtaining an ID card. We can advocate for reasonable treatment by the police and courts on their behalf. We can be nice to them, and pray with them. We can honor them as fellow men and women, by asking them to tell us the lessons they have learned in their hard lives. We can learn from their unfortunate mistakes. They are more than willing to share their stories.

Remember that Jesus himself was a homeless man without a place to lay his head at night. He was speaking from first-hand experience when he spoke of the simple act of giving a cup of water to one of His little ones. It wasn't theory. He had been there many times on his itinerant journeys through Judea, Samaria, and the region east of the Sea of Galilee. His disciples were instructed to travel lightly on their itinerant healing and teaching journeys. No extra tunics, no extra sandals, only one staff and one sword (interesting), and without any money. Jesus' disciples, too, traveled like homeless men and women. Can there be any doubt that Jesus is the friend of the homeless? Can there be any doubt that He desires to "use" His disciples to meet the needs of the homeless? When we touch the homeless, we touch someone dear to Jesus' heart.

THE PARADOX OF A SOUND MIND

To some people in despair under a dark cloud of hopelessness, it would seem logical to them that their circumstances could not get any worse. Consider the title of this book and place an emphasis on one of its terms, *Hope When Everything SEEMS Hopeless*. Many times the situation is not hopeless, but it *seems* to us that it is. Our *perception* of our personal "reality" is the issue. Folks, it might not be that bad in fact, yet we overemphasize the negative aspects of our problem in our own minds. What seems "real" isn't always as bad as it appears to our way of thinking. For instance, we might not know the full picture. Or, even if we know the full picture, our circumstances could change in the future. Time has a way of invading our static view of a crisis. We can't stop time, and with it will come some measure of change, ranging from inconsequential to a breakthrough.

Life does not consist of only our one perceived "reality" at that moment. What seems real on the surface to an individual at that moment might not even be reality. We might misunderstand our circumstances, or be deceived by information or others, or not have Heaven's perspective on the whole picture. There might be other "realities" that we have not considered. There might be a better heavenly reality just waiting for someone to seize upon it. God could be waiting patiently for someone with an effective prayer life or the gift of faith to step up. Maybe the Creator has a long-duration master plan to impact the seemingly hopeless situation or to use it for a greater glory at a later time. Jesus did that when he healed people who had suffered for many years…in one case after 38 years.

Hopeless situations can be the incubator for a great testimony. What you see is not always what you get! Even the Apostle Paul when facing an imminent shipwreck kept clinging on to faith. But, when his prophetic warnings were not headed by the ship's crew and severe weather prevailed for many days he wrote, *"…we finally gave up all hope of being saved."* (Acts 27:20). Immediately thereafter an angel came to encourage and reassure him of the reality of his future testimony in Rome. Remember this, *"For my [God's] thoughts are not your thoughts, neither are your ways my ways…As the heavens are higher than the earth, so are my ways higher than your ways and my thoughts than your thoughts."* (Isaiah 55:8-9). Our perception of "reality" is often missing the mark. This is especially true when we become despondent and depressed in the grip of hopelessness. We just don't think soundly.

Scripture admonishes us to think soundly and with solid doctrine (e.g., see Romans 12:3; 2 Timothy 1:3-7; 2 Timothy 4:1-5, esp. vs. 3). However, ironically walking with a Biblical "sound mind" is a paradox (i.e., two things that don't seem to fit together). Living a Biblical worldview is an uneasy walk upon a pair of parallel rails of a railroad. On one side is *rationality* that brings along with it logic, analysis, prudence, and discipline. On the other side is *faith* that often appears irrational, ridiculous, and mystical as it seeks to "see" and walk into the unseen realm. In order to please God we must demonstrate genuine faith (i.e., Hebrews 11:6). We must cling on to faith, yet while not dropping the other baton of prudent rational thought. We must learn to walk upon these two "opposites", *rational thought* and *Spirit-led faith,* in parallel. And, it is an uncomfortable tandem journey.

Added to this complexity and odd juxtaposition is a major test – *faith* and *presumption* also walk side-by-side like close cousins. We desire faith, but presumption can be misleading. Faith reaches far beyond the grasp of rational thought. Anyone who desires to live a life of faith cannot remain anchored *only* in rational thought. This is a common tendency among Evangelicals. Faith has the ability to "see" into the future and to live as if it were already appropriated for today. And, without *hope* one cannot have any faith. The sequence is hope, then faith, in order to be pleasing to God.

Many agnostics, atheists, and academics would presume that it is impossible for a research scientist to be a *man of faith*, while working in a secular analytical scientific environment that embraces only rational thought. Yet, I say to you confidently as both a scientist and a *man of faith*, we must cling to both rails at the same time. Regardless of the apparent paradox, we must hold on to *rationality* and to *faith*, without letting go of either one. That is the essence of walking with a sound mind and embracing a greater "reality". And, it is the basis upon which sound doctrine is established.

[Note to self: These are *deep crying unto deep* insights. These concepts are difficult to grasp without the revelation of the Holy Spirit.]

A POTENTIAL SCENARIO OF FUTURE ADVERSITY

But, it could get far worse! To further dramatize this point, consider the following possible scenario (and please be mindful that this document was completed in mid-2007). Just imagine you're a resident of the USA and that all or most of the following adversities happened in short order:

- Russia's leadership agrees to strategically "marry" another nation in an alliance. They have two choices, resembling Rachel and Leah before Jacob. One is very desirable, the other less so. But, in expediency Russia quickly makes an alliance with another nation, perhaps Iran. Then, "all hell breaks loose". Like a brute on a sandy beach, muscles are flexed. Military actions will soon become a reality. The world becomes a less stable place in a matter of months.

- Anti-Semitism, Neo-Nazism, and opposition toward the Anointed One (Jesus) and toward genuine Christians builds toward a crescendo in Central Europe. False accusations of the innocent become commonplace and they are targeted for persecution. Another holocaust like the one during WWII occurs in the German-speaking portions of Central Europe. People are shot, run over by vehicles, and burned to death in their homes, yet while other pedestrians walk by indifferent to the malicious treatment. The accused are corralled into camps where they must lay on snow-covered ground in man-made graves. It is most cost-effective to kill the prisoners this way. Another Central European Holocaust has begun.

- China rapidly ascends as a leading Superpower nation. China takes control over the USA financially, but shortly thereafter decides it is to their strategic advantage to assert greater control over America using their massive military. After all, they can out-man the current US military by several hundred Chinese soldiers per each American soldier. So, Chinese troops and tanks roll down the avenues of Washington, DC and New York City. The ability to speak Mandarin Chinese becomes a most valuable skill.

- The *Global Islamic War* has escalated and destabilized many nations around the globe. The Islamists' possession of weapons of mass destruction are no longer doubted, for they have and will use them freely in acts of hatred, and perhaps in a prominent US city like Philadelphia for instance.

- The economy of the USA collapses, so that the former presumptions of what has value are turned upside down. Retirement accounts are worthless or nearly so. Farmers in the heartland of the Great Plains and South who own farmland now have greater influence, as the "new" economy is agro-centric. Those who were formerly highly-paid bankers, lawyers, technology geeks, insurance brokers, advertisers, and stock brokers in the cities lose their controlling influence over the economy, and many despair of their great loss of wealth.

- Safe transportation by air, road, or rail becomes increasingly difficult. Fuel is difficult to obtain as supply chains are disrupted. Bicycles and motor scooters are in demand so much that they are routinely stolen. In some places, bicycles are worth more that a used car.

- Untainted clean water and energy alternatives become highly prized. The high cost of heating a home will drive families to share a single home rather than heating two of them.

- No one takes for granted anymore that medications will be available. Those dependent upon expensive therapies will suffer, as access to medications and medical care become difficult. The days of presuming that we can easily obtain eye glasses for the myopic or insulin for diabetics will be a distant memory.

- Demonic spirits of *confusion* and *hopelessness* become manifest like a pandemic affecting most families. Individuals think they are becoming paranoid, and there are many valid reasons to be paranoid. And if you are not paranoid, you become concerned that everyone around you is becoming paranoid. Everyone is concerned that other people have weapons and that they are irrational, which in turn feeds more paranoia. Fear is rampant. There seems to be no safe place to hide.

- The media provide increasingly gloomy reports of various catastrophes. And, that is when one can obtain any news at all.

- Anarchy is near the door. Except for the limited military police presence, it would be chaos.

- And worst of all, it appears that none of your prayers are answered! When you need Him the most, it seems that God is not listening.

Well then, what would you do about this potential prescient crisis if it happens? If this type of scenario, in whole or in part, were to play out in the USA's future, where would you find hope and solace? Would you still trust in the Lord God of Israel? Would you still seek out a local church congregation (that is, if they were permitted by the ruling government)?

In a parallel to this scenario, have you ever meditated on the impact of the Assyrians' attack on Israel, followed shortly thereafter by the Babylonian's attack on Judah? The Hebrews' circumstances would have produced many of the same fears as the scenario portrayed above. But note that God Himself in His sovereignty prepared Israel and Judah for captivity in the East in advance. Just look at what He said in advance through His trusted prophets. He even reminded Daniel (in Daniel 9) seventy years into the Babylonian captivity that He had written before the captivity, *"For I know the plans I have for you...plans to prosper you and not to harm you, plans to give you hope and a future."* (Jeremiah 29:11).

God's plan was to chastise Israel and Judah for idolatry, disbelief, and other sins. But, He showed mercy even in judgment. God desired for a good outcome by the future remnant. He instructed them to settle down, be industrious, and be fruitful during their 70-year captivity. During that season the Lord would rebuild His chosen remnant. God's rhema word via Jeremiah in advance prepared them to have an attitude of hope in the midst of their long trial in a foreign land.

MARRIAGE ON THE ROCKS OR BUILT ON THE ROCK?

Marital stresses can be one of life's greatest challenges. Pressures of finances, lost love, pursuit of selfish desires, and other worries have taken a toll on many marriages. In our Western society, we've abandoned the wisdom of the ages and have embraced divorce as the easy-out option. Half of marriages in the States end on the rocks. Why is this the case, and what can be done to stop this trend?

In the West many of us don't honor our commitments. We even counsel people to break their own promises out of convenience and the avoidance of pain. When we divorce our spouse we become *covenant breakers*, and this brings curses upon us (2 Samuel 21). These curses will deny us from maximal blessings in our future, and can have adverse effects on our offspring, and potentially for several generations to come.

Even if it *seems* right to divorce, it *seldom* is right. Even the Biblical exception probably only applied to a unique condition within Hebrew marital culture during the pre-consummation betrothal stage of their tradition. It should be extremely difficult to break a covenant bond. Yet, when I ponder the ease at which people enter into divorces today in the West I am mindful of: *"There is a way that seems right to a man, but in the end it leads to death."* (Proverbs 14:12); and *"All a man's ways seem innocent to him, but motives are weighed by the Lord."* (Proverbs 16:2). Our "heart" can be very deceptive, and especially when we're attempting to avoid pain.

We can convince our minds that any disgusting food tastes sweet when we're famished. When we want out of a relationship, by golly we want out! We will even change our prior theological opinions that prohibited the behavior, so as to conform to our new desires. Bill Gothard taught that *"a man's morality dictates his theology."* If you want to do something strongly, you will find justification for it. You'll also surround yourself by those who agree with you, so as to avoid the guilt and shame associated with the divorce. This principle applies beyond the issue of divorce. It doesn't matter what one's "sin of choice" might be – this pattern still applies (i.e. changing your theology and seeking those to affirm your decision).

The hard Biblical truth is that God expects us to maintain our pledge of covenant in marriage. "Covenant" is not an easy word. Unfortunately, the term "covenant" is flippantly tossed around today by many Charismatics and Pentecostals, and in a manner that diminishes its superlative value. It demands full submission of our will to honor our covenant. It's terms cannot be broken, except upon death. God says, for this reason a man and woman shall be united into one new family unit. Therefore, what God has put together in the bond of marriage, let no man separate...and that includes the husband, wife, and any third party advising or seeking to promote a divorce. If the marriage situation is extremely unsafe or difficult, then separation might be suitable.

God says that He <u>hates</u> divorce (read Malachi 2, I Corinthians 7, Mark 10, Matthew 5, and Matthew 19). In this context, just look at the distinction between what God says that He *commands* of us in obedience versus what He *permits* out of the hardness of men's hearts. Therefore, anyone toying with divorce is essentially thinking, *"I like the idea of divorce more than the person I've married. My covenant vows are less important to me than my current desire to get out. I don't want covenant, I want convenient. Therefore, I now like what God hates.*" May that not be true of any genuine obedient disciple of Jesus.

We shall be judged in the heavenly realm for whether we kept our most important earthly covenant. And, marriage vows are the most important earthly vow we can make. The fabric of society is built upon the merits of a covenant-based decree. The family unit is established upon that oath, and the family is the building block of civil and spiritual society. This is critically important! That is why the devil works so hard to destroy marriages, or produce counterfeits (e.g., living together or homosexual "marriages"). Without solid marriages the fabric of moral society collapses. Therefore, goals for a married couple should include: (1) To honor the covenant vows that were established before witnesses on earth and in the spiritual heavenly realm; (2) To keep the marriage on the ROCK, the solid foundation of Jesus; (3) To pray for repentance, restitution, and deliverance when encountering hardships; (4) To pray and declare God's intended abundant blessings on the marriage and family to be bearing much fruit.

Then only in extreme cases (e.g., grossly irresponsible behavior, such as physical violence) should one seek to leave one's spouse. While separated, one should endure the difficulties knowing that His grace is sufficient for you.

Here are some additional thoughts for those who are enduring a difficult marriage and might be contemplating divorce: (1) The principle of *reaping what we sow* is true. If we were unwise in our selection of a spouse, or didn't work on the marriage, then we'll reap what we have sown. It is unavoidable. If the marriage is not a high priority, then it will decay into a shambles infested with rat holes; (2) The media, music industry, and higher education have done an effective job of destroying the concept of *covenant of marriage*. They have introduced to people various avenues of convenient sin. They are flaunting sin every hour of every day. They are declaring, *"Here's a get-out-of-jail-free-card...it is easy to get a divorce...everyone is doing it...you deserve a better life!"* We must make conscious efforts to avoid it. We must choose to run away from these evil influences. And, (3) God expects submission and obedience from His disciples, and He has the right to expect it. After all the Cross of Calvary was very expensive. Our happiness is not where He places much, if any, emphasis. Yes, He loves us. Yes, He wants to bless us. But, He also disciplines us for our own good and for the good of our society. Those of us living in the West need to grow up, and to return to sound Biblical instruction on the *covenant of marriage*.

You might think that I have touched upon a sacred cow that just shouldn't be discussed in a book on the topic of hope. You might be thinking, I was already depressed before reading this section. What joy does one get out of being reminded of the problem? Before we as either married or divorced individuals can be restored, we must first repent. Repentance is painful as it exposes our problems to the light of His grace and the Spirit's consuming fire. Jesus said that a house built upon a foundation of sand will eventually collapse. I am convinced that there is a major devilish attack against the family and starting at its core, the *covenant of marriage*. Until we get this point restored within the Body of Christ, all that we are doing will be like rearranging deck chairs on the Titanic. There can be no real hope unless we embrace sound doctrine concerning the *covenant of marriage*, and then work hard at maintaining solid marriages. If you want hope, then return to *truth in love*. Anything less will not bring about real hope.

FACING THE BATTLES

When I think of the word "depressing", I sometimes ponder men in their late teens and twenties heading off to war in a foreign land. One example to illuminate our understanding of war is the poem *Dulce et Decorum est* by Wilfred Owen, the most famous poet of World War I:

> *Bent double, like old beggars under sacks,*
> *Knock-kneed, coughing like hags, we cursed through sludge,*
> *Till on the haunting flares we turned our backs*
> *And towards our distant rest began to trudge.*
> *Men marched asleep. Many had lost their boots*
> *But limped on, blood-shod. All went lame; all blind;*
> *Drunk with fatigue; deaf even to the hoots*

Of disappointed shells that dropped behind.

Gas! Gas! Quick, boys! – An ecstasy of fumbling,
Fitting the clumsy helmets just in time;
But someone still was yelling out and stumbling
And floundering like a man in fire or lime.–
Dim, through the misty panes and thick green light
As under a green sea, I saw him drowning.
In all my dreams, before my helpless sight,
He plunges at me, guttering, choking, drowning.

If in some smothering dreams you too could pace
Behind the wagon that we flung him in,
And watch the white eyes writhing in his face,
His hanging face, like a devil's sick of sin;
If you could hear, at every jolt, the blood
Come gargling from the froth-corrupted lungs,
Obscene as cancer, bitter as the cud
Of vile, incurable sores on innocent tongues,–
My friend, you would not tell with such high zest
To children ardent for some desperate glory,
The old Lie: Dulce et decorum est
Pro patria mori.

The translation of "the old lie" from Latin is *"How sweet and noble it is to die for one's country"*. Patriotism can have some temporary and even possibly long-term benefits. Yet, death on some foreign field raises the question of how valuable is patriotism. It is finality for the young man who gave his last breath. Is patriotism worth dying for? How can a man find any hope in a battlefield scenario like this one?

I have a deep regard for the men and women of uniform. I occasionally pray inside of the Pentagon with officers, as well as with individual soldiers or sailors I might encounter in my journeys. At times I have had to share with some of them "hard" words about current crises in the world and about what I "see" that is coming in the days ahead. I have a deep respect and gratitude for the military. Their prior actions have secured for me my current breath!

Those fighting in foreign campaigns have so much at risk. [Us "soft-ies" remaining in comfort at home can barely imagine it.] Decisions made by their superiors and colleagues in the field can cost them life, or limb, or even result indirectly in the break up of a marriage. A young man filled with ambition, confidence, and capabilities can go into war and later returned home in a wheelchair or a body bag. Or while he's away the anxiety of the unknown can fester and damage the precious minds of their children.

This is where the rubber meets the road concerning hope or hope-lessness. I believe that there is no greater hope on earth than that which comes from Jesus, the Creator-Son. His hope is superior to any that we can muster. He is the champion of hope. He, who faced death and de-feated it, is the bearer of all genuine hope. He is not afraid of anything or anyone, and His reservoir of hope is without end. It is a deep well. His hope is a substance that He provides to His own through His grace. In times of great challenge to life and limb, a hope that is based upon the in-tellect of mere men is no hope at all. A transcendent hope from Jehovah's Throne in Heaven is what is required. The very hope that overcame the grave is a hope that pierces the darkness of any circumstance in front of us. As purveyors of the Gospel of Peace of Jesus, we have the privilege of presenting to our fellow men and women this hope that is superior to any that we can muster.

HELL – THE ULTIMATE WORST CASE SCENARIO

When you convince yourself that life cannot get any worse, remind yourself of the many blessings surrounding you and those whom you love. Life on earth can throw us many curve balls and in some instances hellish pain, suffering, and persecution. Yet, in all of these cases on earth, there is still at least one reason to rejoice if you are a child of the King of kings and bound for an eternity with Him. Hell is worse that the so-called "hell" one is currently facing here on earth. Hell is real! It is not imaginary, or out-dated, or an old wives' tale. There is always something far worse – an eternal Hell separated from the light and love of the Almighty.

May we do everything in our power to prevent anyone from falling into this dark abyss, where there will be no room for any hope by anyone. The hope of Jesus is all that is needed to prevent someone from going into that dark place. By simply humbling ourselves and repenting of our sins, we can receive forgiveness through Jesus' completed work and be embraced into His heavenly eternity.

8
LEADING WITH HOPE
WHEN FEW FOLLOW

Two centuries ago Napoleon Bonaparte of France declared, "*A leader is a dealer in hope.*" A genuine leader casts a "vision" for the future and seeks to bring his or her plans into reality. If one desires to build a team of followers, hope becomes the glue that holds the followers' attention to that declared vision. Therefore, the leader must project an optimistic image of the future. Unless you're a criminal thug or anarchist, who would want to follow a self-declared "leader", who lacks "vision" or hope? Effective leaders must have a storehouse of hope within them. Scripture tells us that a pupil cannot be greater than one's teacher. Therefore, if the leader doesn't believe in the "vision" and project it as a definite future reality, then the follower certainly won't adopt it either. First and foremost a true leader must have genuine hope themselves, regardless of whether anyone follows them or not. Hope is the starting point in the development of a leader and is among the key resources required for leadership. Leaders must have a reservoir of hope!

THE METRICS OF LEADERSHIP

How should disciples of Jesus today evaluate the effectiveness of leaders or potential leaders? It is routinely declared in contemporary leadership books and conferences that, *"In order to be a leader one must have followers!"* Running in parallel with this statement are two subordinate presumptions: (a) Leadership is measured by "people assets", i.e., those below them, whereas "non-people assets" are considered as less important or unimportant; and (b) *More* followers are better than *fewer*. This principle and its subordinate corollaries are commonly expressed as dogma by contemporary leadership gurus. These remarks are being made from both the secular and religious disciplines. We often hear if from authors of books on leadership as well as from coaches of athletic teams. These comments are presented as authoritative truth, as if it is insight handed down directly by God Almighty.

Although there is *some* merit to this oft-cited simple statement, this remark is misleading. Furthermore, it can be quite discouraging to millions of under-appreciated leaders and leaders-in-training worldwide. This erroneous metric of leadership can damage the establishment of hope within them.

Let me explain. The fundamental inherent flaw in this all-too-common statement is that it presumes that *the* singular hallmark of a leader is equated with the *number of people* who are following the individual at that juncture in time. Where did this presumption come from? Where in the Bible does it equate *de facto* the number of people with "success" as a leader *per se*? Honestly, I cannot find it anywhere in the Bible.

The number of followers is merely one of multiple metrics or measures to assess so-called leadership "success". The number of people is only *one* metric upon which leadership capabilities are quantifiable. Even then, it can often be a misleading metric. The problem is that there are many metrics by which a leader can be judged, and the number of followers is only one of many metric indices. If the emphasis is always on the number of followers *per se*, then by that standard Adolf Hitler was a highly effective leader. Chairman Mao Zedong was also a highly effective leader. Yet, it can be argued that being effective at garnering a large number of followers does not equate with being a "good" leader (and certainly not from a Biblical perspective). Both of these men were responsible for horrible atrocities, yet while being considered as highly effective leaders based upon the metric of "number of followers".

Please permit me to clarify other ways to discern a genuine leader, and especially from a Kingdom of God perspective. Genuine leaders come in various and sundry types of personalities, professions, natural talents, and spiritual gifts (both the natural and supernatural types). They can lead in various capacities and many, if not most, of these realms are not measurable by the mere number of followers. We have had too much of the world's tainted views of leadership cast upon the Judeo-Christian realm in recent years. The "bigger is better" and "more is better" movement has effectively crept into the Christian leadership circles.

Let us consider various examples demonstrating how this misleading teaching limits a God-honoring broad perspective of what quality leadership really means. Let's first start with the typical obvious cases from the Judeo-Christian ministry world in which the number of people appears to be equated with leadership potential. Typical examples include pastors or teaching elders who are entrusted with the oversight of a congregation. It is unfortunately common for people to judge by the natural *eyes of sight* the number of people attending a service, and they inappropriately draw conclusions about the effectiveness of the pastor's leadership capacities. Such simple judgments are incomplete, imprecise, and in some cases totally incorrect.

Does it always mean that if a pastor provides care for a relatively small home-based "church" with only 15 people attending in a rural remote environment or a small Native American-style *Talking Circle*, that the pastor is *less* of a *spiritual* leader than a super-star pastor of a megachurch in affluent suburban USA with a multi-million dollar budget and thousands of people in attendance? Isn't it possible that in some cases the leader with fewer folks is actually a better *spiritual* leader than the one with more folks. The latter could be merely an effective *worldly* leader, who might have made compromises to be more attractive and appealing to an audience? Isn't it probable that in some instances the reduced number of people actually reflects the fact that the leader is *more* obedient to God's leading and he exhibits genuine *fear of the Lord*? When he preaches he delivers the *whole counsel of the Lord*, not some watered-down baby food that tickles the ears of listeners to entertain them. Whereas, on the contrary the leader with many followers might actually be displaying a character flaw by exhibiting the *fear of man*, so as to be pleasing to the largest possible audience. Perhaps that latter pastor has an issue with pride, or building an empire for his career success, or is in venomous competition with other pastors in that region. Please listen! There are plenty of examples in the Bible where the hallmarks of a *spiritual* leader were defined as the exact opposite of someone amassing a large number of followers. We'll look at several Biblical examples further below.

Let's take this to the extreme to further make the point. What if one of the "most numerically successful" pastors or evangelists made an intentional career change at the prompting of the Holy Spirit? He decided to "down-size" from a large ministry of drawing thousands of followers, so as to not merely collect a lot of pew-sitters or produce a whole lot of new *believers*. Rather, he chose to focus strategically on investing all of his wisdom and spiritual gifts into only 12 people – one dozen chosen "green" *disciples*.

God desires for Christ-likeness to become fully manifest in all of us as we undergo the transformations from unsaved *non-believer* to saved *believer*, and then from *believer* to obedient *disciple*. The first transformation centers on Jesus as *Savior*, whereas the second transformation centers on Jesus as *Lord* or boss. So, this leader with a new outlook is no longer preaching or teaching to thousands of people on a regular basis, he is intentionally maximizing his time with only 12 chosen individuals. Now, is this man wise for down sizing to be obedient to the Holy Spirit's leading? Is he *less* of a leader now, than he was when he oversaw the evangelism and teaching of thousands of people? Certainly not! But, the *carnal* observer might say, *"What a pity. He's wasting his career and leadership potential on a pathetically small group."* But, that is just an expression of seeing only by the *eyes of sight* with a worldly perspective.

It is often an error to equate the number of followers with the measure of a leader's capacity or character. The example of Ernest Shackleton, the commander of the *Endurance* journey (back in Chapter 2), is an example of a man having few followers, but with phenomenal leadership ability. Jesus, too, invested the majority of his ministry time into the lives of a small cadre of a dozen male disciples. He placed even greater emphasis on only three of the men, who belonged to an inner core of trusted passionate friends, the impulsive Simon Peter and the two *Sons of Thunder* brothers, James and John. Sure, on selected occasions He preached to the masses of thousands and healed many of them of various diseases and cast out demons. But, His heart's mission was focused more intensely on discipling this core group of 12 and especially the inner core group of three. Jesus was a great leader and He was not judging by the carnal eyes of sight. Based upon Jesus as the "Gold Standard" of Biblical leadership, it suggests that the premise of judging leaders by the number of followers is off track.

Consider another typical and faulty example of modern ministries. A woman is a successful marketing manager in a commercial advertising firm, and is responsible for many big corporate accounts. She joins as a "member" of a local church, even though she doesn't know Jesus in a personal relationship. She has not repented and is therefore not *born again*. She just thinks it is a good idea to have her children become involved in some Sunday school programs with religious teachings, in the hopes of building up a "good moral foundation" for her kids.

When the church's leadership team learned about her professional accomplishments in the secular advertising world, they enthusiastically presume that she will be an excellent leader of a new program to advertise and promote their "church" to the region. After all, they believe that they need to "grow" or else they won't be able to service the debt obligations on their new elegant facilities' mortgage. So, she uses her knowledge of *worldly* advertising campaigns and is effective at drawing in an additional six percent into membership that year. The financial contributions increase, more than offsetting the cost of the advertising campaign budget. The church's leadership team is elated with the "numbers" and then promotes her to a position of high *spiritual authority* of governance within this local congregation (e.g., elder status). They compliment themselves and her declaring, *"She's a productive leader!"* Yet, the entire time, she has not become a *believer* in Jesus, and without being a believer she can't be a *disciple*. And without being a disciple, she certainly can't be a genuine *spiritual* leader. She just used her *worldly* skills, albeit applied to a non-secular arena. This is an application of professional talent without God's anointing or methods.

What is wrong with this all-to-common scenario in a typical Western church? The church's leadership team (the pastor, the staff, and/or the elders) is judging by the natural *eyes of sight*, and not by the discerning of the Holy Spirit through the *eyes of faith*. This woman had apparent *worldly* success, and was termed as an effective "leader". But, she was <u>not</u> an effective *spiritual* leader from God's perspective. She was a dangerous "misleader" from the Kingdom's perspective! Fully aided by the church's leadership team, she could be engrafted into leadership as a "wolf in sheep's clothing". The leadership team acted irresponsibly, yet were well pleased with their actions. She was spiritually disqualified from the start, and should have never been chosen for this strategic advertising campaign for the purpose of increasing numbers. Even the goal of a "marketing campaign" itself raises some concern...that's worthy of consideration beyond the scope of this book. Don't confuse *worldly* leadership with *spiritual* leadership! Spiritual leadership must flow out of the Spirit and the methods and wisdom of God. Let's not take the "good" business practices of the world, dress them up with a Bible verse or two, and then spin the whole thing as God's way forward! Yet, this very thing is happening all the time in ministries...judging by the natural rather than by the spiritual perspective.

SPIRITUAL LEADERSHIP WITHIN THE KINGDOM OF GOD

I have observed throughout my professional career (as a scientist, entrepreneur, professor, and businessman) and ministry roles, that we should look beyond this misleading principle of judging a potential leader based on the number of people following him or her. It is too simplistic. I don't believe that it is supported by the Scriptures.

May I suggest for your consideration the following alternative principles? The first principle of an effective spiritual leader or leader-in-training should be, *"Do you <u>hear</u> clearly the voice of God?"* The second principle is connected to it, *"Do you quickly <u>obey</u> the voice of God?"* Those who hear His rhema given by the Spirit and obey the promptings are leaders on the advancing frontlines of the Kingdom. They are *de facto* leading the way. All others are mere followers, and regardless of the number of people hanging around them. A leader is on the front lines. They hear the commander's voice during the battle. They see the battle immediately ahead of them. It is our Lord's desire that we hear and quickly obey His voice.

Why do I propose this alternative to conventional wisdom? First of all, *natural* leaders are not *spiritual* leaders. In John chapter 3 Jesus spoke of being "born of the Spirit" as an otherworldly experience. Within the Kingdom of God, a standard of a leader from God's perspective is quickly obeying His commands. He's looking for *proven character* and someone that He can trust. The Scriptures indicate that our character is demonstrated through love, which is an expression of obeying His will. In the Kingdom of God, unless specifically directed otherwise, the numbers of people (or resources) *per se* are of secondary importance, and sometimes are of no value whatsoever.

Whereas, in the world measures of productivity (i.e., number of followers, results, revenue, increases, etc.) are touted as supreme standards. In the world a man or woman can be carnal, corrupt, dishonest, manipulative, selfish, proud, controlling, and of reprobate character…so long as they deliver results. Folks, I hear and see this all the time in the marketplace…I'm in their arena all the time.

This utilitarian concept is often today unfortunately being applied within local churches and ministries, as they strive for numerical growth as the supreme ideal. Since when has *quantity* become the measure of Biblical virtue? I'm definitely in favor of growth for the advancement of the Kingdom of God, but not merely growth for growth's sake. In large part the focus of evangelism and discipleship should be one of quality, not quantity. When walking in relationship with the Living Lord (Adonai), what He wants from us is seldom ever what the world wants from us. He is often not interested in the numbers, results, or activities *per se*, but rather in the quality of the character that is being formed within the disciple.

Parenthetically, I would rather have one serious and devoted disciple as a trusted friend, than a small army of mere believers as followers. In the *Great Commission,* Jesus said that we are to make *disciples* of all the nations, who *obey* all of His commands, not mere *believers* (Matt. 28:18-20; emphasis added). Disciples are characterized by a pattern of obedience to Jesus. Oh! When did we lose the focus on the Biblical meaning of faith, converting it from "risk-taking belief in action" into mere mental assent or belief without requiring any action of real consequence? What a tragedy. It is one thing to believe something, it is quite another to be obedient with your feet in response to the belief. And that is a fundamental difference between a mere *believer* and a true *disciple.*

The disciple lives by genuine faith and is surrendered, whereas the mere believer is still in control of his or her own life. The mere believer lives a compromised milk toast lifestyle of *"me plus pleasant thoughts of Jesus"*. I find no evidence that this latter type of philosophy pays honor to the high cost of God's saving grace. Just thinking nice thoughts about Jesus, but not obeying Him, is a serious crisis affecting perhaps the majority of believers today in Western "churchianity".

My friends, mere belief alone doesn't cut it with God Almighty! He expects far more from us. He expects us to surrender our will and actions to the King of kings, and say *"Yes, sir. Reporting for duty."* Jesus saw the hypocrisy in people saying to Him, *"Lord, Lord"*. He sternly rebuked them with *"Why do you call me 'Lord, Lord', and not do what I tell you to do?"* If He is Lord, then you will do what He wants. If He is not Lord, then you won't. This isn't rocket science. The Lordship of Jesus is at the crossroads between being a disciple vs. a mere believer.

El Shaddai is concerned about our ability to *listen* carefully to His voice and to quickly *obey* what He is saying. Just ponder Jesus as the ultimate spiritual leader. He did so by following His Father's voice. Jesus never did anything without first hearing what His Father was saying or seeing what His Father was doing (refer to the Gospel of John). Please listen to this very important Biblical truth! The first step in being a spiritual leader in the Kingdom of God is to be an effective listener and follower of the Holy Spirit's voice. Those who hear His *rhema* revelation, or in other words the "now" Word of God, will be the most effective at prophetically discerning where God intends to move next (Amos 3:7). If you want to be on the *cutting edge* as an effective spiritual leader, you must be in close relationship with the Lord and know what His plans are for the future. If you don't have God's current plans for you, then you'll be operating in "yesterday's anointing" or presumption.

The individual who has received God's rhema revelation for the "now" season must then be *obedient* to follow through in action. And in order to have the "privilege" to listen to his voice on the mountain, a disciple must be following the path of righteousness (Psalm 24; Isaiah 62). You are disqualified from being a genuine spiritual leader if you do not do these two things, namely (a) hear His voice, and (b) obey it quickly! That is what makes you a spiritual leader...one who is out in front and doing what God wants done at the right time. Anyone who fails at either of these criteria, is either a false/presumptuous leader or a follower. Think about it!

Let's consider the lives of just a few of the greatest spiritual leaders of the Hebrew Bible, as they stood firm in faith even though few followed them:

DAVID

As a small boy and the youngest sibling, he demonstrated almost supernatural courage and composure as he single-handedly confronted the Philistine giant. David had already been tested in small ways while working with his family's flock. But, his larger-than-life demonstration proved the heart of a God-fearing leader. He had no *fear of man* when countering Goliath's mocking of the True Living God. This demonstrates nothing less than exceptional leadership. No one supported him, and his own elder brother mocked him to his face.

One of the concerns that I recognize in many *platform* ministers (i.e., those who hold the microphone) is that they are often out-of-balance concerning the *fear of man*. Whether this is out of concern for financial security, the need to be affirmed and appreciated by the masses, the need to have his or her *ego* stroked, false humility, or whatever the rationale, the *fear of man* is a nasty destructive force that drains the blood of genuine faith from a minister. If you are afraid of man, you do not fear God. If you are afraid of man, you fear the devil. From my perspective, David had no fear of man within him, even as a small shepherd boy. [He had to learn faith that pushes through fears.] This is a hallmark of a genuine spiritual man or woman – one who fears God more than he fears man! Show me someone who has the faith (i.e., risk-taking belief in action) of David today, and I'll show you a great spiritual leader, regardless of the number of followers. To my way of understanding, a man or woman of genuine faith is a leader on the frontlines of the Kingdom of God.

JOSEPH

There are at least two alternative interpretations of Joseph's motives for revealing his revelations from God via dreams, when he told his half-brothers about his future as a leader to whom they would be subordinated.

The most commonly mentioned interpretation weighs heavily upon the immaturity of a *young boy*, aged 17. This interpretation speculates and implies that Joseph was impulsive, boastful, and spoiled in view of his special "favored" status in the eyes of his father. *[Note there is no explicit evidence of this in Scripture. It is inferred by interpretation. And, for what it is worth I don't find compelling support for this interpretation. It is a case of the "eye of the beholder" perspective of some readers. It might be true, but the evidence is based upon speculation and is sketchy.]*

The actions by Joseph and his brothers were in large part due to their father's favoritism toward Joseph, which in turn was due to Jacob's genuine love for Rachel, who bore Joseph and Benjamin. So, a lot of what happened to and through Joseph was due to the favor and sovereign will of the Heavenly Father, who orchestrated the entire symphony of relationships!

The alternative interpretation is that as a *young prophet*, Joseph was making a prophetic declaration about certain events in the future. He did so courageously in spite of the consequences to himself at the time. This alternative interpretation is reasonable, because there is no *explicit* mention of "sin" by Joseph in the account of his interaction with his brothers, who were definitely nasty dudes. Furthermore, prophets are often *required* to make declarations of future events, and at considerable risk to themselves. Without the declarations in advance, anyone could question the prediction's validity later.

Joseph's prophetic life portrays an excellent *Christophany*, a cinematic preview of Jesus' life. In view of Joseph's prophetic calling in life, it is reasonable that what he did were acts of obedience as a young prophet before his brothers and father. Just as in the case of David, no one supported Joseph, and his own elder brothers mocked him to his face. Joseph stood alone! Yet, he was absolutely precisely *right* concerning the prophetic revelations of the future, and his actions resulted in the ultimate elevation of him as a forerunner leader of the future Hebrew nation.

As a prophetic individual myself I can clearly see the prophetic nature of Joseph's actions (even if they possibly involved a bit of immaturity during his youth). You can't really appreciate and understand Joseph's motivation and actions in making prescient predictions, if you have never walked in that type of prophetic anointing and the *favor of the Lord*.

I've observed the favor of the Lord in the life of Shaun Alexander, the running back for the Seattle Seahawks professional football team. He was the *right man*, in the *right place*, at the *right time*. Shaun had all three necessary ingredients to maximize God's anointing upon his life. He was prepared and his anointing by the favor of God opened a door of opportunity at a key juncture. He has been a remarkable record-setting running back in high school, at the University of Alabama, and at the professional level in Seattle. He became one of the elite few to receive the Most Valuable Player (MVP) Award of the National Football League (NFL). In addition, he is a man of honorable, altruistic, Judeo-Christian character both on and off the playing field. We need more motivational spiritual leaders like Shaun, who carry a Joseph-like anointing in their profession.

JOSHUA & CALEB

Decades before either man was promoted to a central role in the leadership of the nascent Hebrew nation, these men were tested under fire to prove their merit. No one followed them. Yet, when twelve men were sent in to do reconnaissance within Canaan, only two – Joshua and Caleb, trusted the revealed Word of the Lord about the assured outcome of victory. Only two stood on God's side, and the other ten plus essentially all of the mass of people rose to attack them. This is one of the finest examples of genuine spiritual leadership in the Hebrew Scriptures, and yet no one was following their correct spiritual leadership! In this case the masses were all wrong. The masses are often wrong. The majority is often wrong. So, in the case when the majority is wrong or impure, having a large following is a detriment, rather than a sign of a great leader.

ESTHER & MORDECAI

There is little evidence that Esther and Mordecai had a great following. They operated in relative obscurity *until* the day that God chose to elevate them to prominence. But all the while their character was being refined in preparation for a key moment in history. Let us not despise the days of small beginnings. At the right time, both individuals were elevated to prominence, and their obedient leadership helped preserve the entire Hebrew nation.

Leadership is metered differently for various types of life callings. A leader who is called as a pastor or apostle probably will have a numerical following. But, what about an intercessor, who focuses on prayer alone or with a few others, or a worshipper, who choreographs dance, or a prophet, who spends time recording revelations in journals to share at an appropriate time, or an artist, who captures a new genre of expression of a truth for others to view? All of them can be on the cutting edge of what God is speaking to them in rhema revelation. They are on the front lines of God's movements, and far ahead of others who aren't rhema-led, albeit coincidentally have a bunch of followers. Of all the leaders in ministry only a few callings can be assessed or monitored based on the number of followers. This is so obvious, yet it is overlooked and/or suppressed by those in control. Please don't discourage those who have few "followers" at present. They might well be smack dab in the middle of God's will for them in leadership!

LONE RANGERS – LEADERS IN THE MARKETPLACE:

Does not even the secular world tells us that one can be an effective leader without many followers? Consider the following types of leaders who are <u>not</u> recognized by followers:

A creative artist introduces a new genre of sculpture, yet is disregarded or chastised by the masses and the professional critics, who coincidentally are considered as the co-called "leaders" of the day. Only toward the end of his or her career or after he or she dies does the artist receive any recognition by "followers", and perhaps posthumously. He or she has forged a way where none have passed before with a new perspective on materials and composition. They resemble the Hebrew prophets who were all killed by the religious leaders of their day. To my way of thinking, this type of artist serves as a genuine leader! A God-led artist can be as valuable or even more valuable to the Kingdom than a pastor, especially if the pastor is more interested in building up his own 'kingdom' with many followers than supporting the true Kingdom of God.

Scientists or engineers labors away for years on key discoveries and inventions. No one pays any attention to them. Their federal research grant requests are denied by the so-called "leaders" of the day. Their manuscripts are often rejected for publication by their competitive peers. They are criticized for not having a better resumé. They are passed over for positions and promotions, only to be assigned a low-visibility low-salaried career. Yet, their discoveries are myriad and dramatically impact the quality of our daily lives. They've discovered new drugs and therapies, improved consumer products, and designed electronic devices for aircraft navigation systems. They were the *first* in the world to observe the result of a key biomedical experiment, or to design a novel mechanical device, or to write the code for a computer software application. To my way of thinking, they are genuine leaders, yet working in near isolation!

A rancher each morning mounts his favorite horse. He rides over many miles across the grazing land to inspect his herd of thousands of cattle in the northwestern hills of the United States. He has little direct contact with the outside world, except when he drives the 50 miles to the nearest market town, where he periodically auctions some of his cattle to the highest bidder. If it were not for this hard working disciplined man leading his family financially, emotionally, and spiritually, where would our society be today? Who would provide the meat to consumers? He's a productive business owner. He is doing an extremely valuable job, yet it is done without any recognition. He might even endure some unde-served criticism as an "uneducated cowboy" by the so-called city dwellers. His numerous tasks and hard work are seldom noticed by anyone. Yet, his family sells hundreds of beef cattle into the marketplace each year pumping dollars into the regional economy. To my way of thinking, this rancher-cowboy is a fine example of a genuine leader!

Finally, consider the ranks of the vast number of entrepreneurs who start small businesses each year. They often have little or no assistance. They have little or no "people assets" reporting to them. But, they have a passion to build upon their "vision" for a successful productive enterprise. Many of them are inventors of new products and services using untested business models. They must learn many diverse skills in order to survive and succeed financially. Typically no one outside of their family, friends, and investors could care a dime whether they succeed or not. They have no followers, until after they are successful. Then, and only then, do folks admire them and write chapters in leadership books based upon testimo-nies of their entrepreneurial success stories. To my way of thinking, they are genuine leaders from the day that they initiate the planning for their new endeavor, and long before anyone cares to follow them!

So, you don't need a following to be a genuine leader in the secular world. The same principle is true in the Kingdom of God. Let's put the myth to rest. A leader can be a "loner" who works diligently toward a goal, with minimal recognition or followers.

THE UNWILLING MANY VS. THE WILLING FEW

There are two very different groups of people within churches. The largest of the two groups consists of the *unwilling many*. They represent a large portion of people, who will *attend* church services. They listen, they ponder, and they might even believe. Then they follow, but only it if suits their personal desires. They are a somewhat pliant bunch as long as they are receiving some chow at the trough. But, they are not surrendered. They really like the social aspects of their local church. They like the sense of belonging, the occasional square dance nights, the potluck meals, and being part of a community of like-minded colleagues.

However, on the other side of the aisle is a smaller group called the *willing few*. It is very difficult to be a leader of the *unwilling many* when one's priority is to be an effective leader of the *willing few*. This latter group is pleased to demonstrate obedience, even if they personally don't benefit or like it. They have been trained to be altruistic and generous in their motives. They are much more in tune with the principles of the Kingdom of Heaven, because they have surrendered. The *willing few* don't need to be sweet-talked, flattered, cajoled, coerced, pushed, or prodded. They have chosen to be obedient and responsible as a part of their character. They've made up their minds that they will live righteously regardless of what others do around them. They'll choose to do the right thing regard-less of whether the crowd cheers or scoffs. George Barna wrote an excellent book about these obedience-prone disciples. It is called <u>Revolution</u>, and I highly recommend it. He speaks of a "remnant" of highly obedient disciples, who remain true regardless of those around them.

Oh that the Lord would raise up even more obedient disciples in our day who would be like salmon swimming upstream to spawn. I've worked several years in Seattle, Washington and have had the opportunity to watch the salmon run in a small stream directly behind my office. My family has also seen them by the hundreds at high density in rivers and streams in Alaska in the late summer.

Salmon have one compelling desire – to be fruitful! They will sacrifice their own bodies to make it to the shallows of their breeding grounds near the headwaters of small streams. While they are struggling to advance miles upstream against rapid currents, some of their peers are dying along the way. There are ample dangers along the way…predators, rocks, and rapids. Yet, they are driven to be fruitful for the sake of the next generation.

If we had obedience, why would there be any "need" to sweet-talk, flatter, cajole, coerce, or prod people into action? Some leaders have no trouble whatsoever with it. For many, it is their primary *modus operandi*. Some leaders have manipulative-controlling "cheerleader" personalities. This style is often sinful and at its root can be demonically enabled. Their ability to draw large crowds and extract financial contributions from followers is directly proportional to their manipulations and personal "charisma". If they ceased to manipulate, they would rapidly lose their followers and finances.

I choose to attempt to lead by example, and trust that potential followers will simply smell the aroma of the food cooking in the kitchen. May the pleasant aroma attract their attention. To the righteous, we should be the fragrant aroma of Christ. If the food isn't aromatic enough, then they won't want to have any part of it. You can either pull 'em or you can push 'em. We need to be very careful not to push people. Servant leaders should have a hard time defending the practice of manipulating others in view of the higher way, the way of the Kingdom of Heaven. *"Not by [your] might, nor by [your] power, but by My Spirit says the Lord"* (a paraphrase of Zechariah 4:6). We need to exhort and admonish, but we cross over a line when we push people. Unfortunately, this manipulative behavior is common with many leaders. I believe that the Almighty desires for them to take their foot off the accelerator pedal and to get out of the driver's seat!

Obedient prophetic and prudent voices speak the things that people don't want to hear. Using the analogy of John-the-baptizer's food (see Matthew 3), those hard words are like bitter grasshoppers, rather than sweet honey. It is easier to be a leader of the *unwilling many*, if you are willing to give them only honey and seldom any grasshoppers. Some ministry leaders have grown huge followings by never speaking anything "negative". Some pastors won't speak on certain Biblical themes, such as repentance. Stroke the *unwilling many* and they'll fall in line. Meet their perceived needs and they'll follow you. Stroke them, pet them, and they'll purr like a kitten. Even a milk cow willingly follows a farmer into the barn to be milked, expecting to get a little corn and hay for her belly. The *unwilling many* occupy huge suburban auditoriums and cathedrals that cater to the desires of so-called "seekers". The *unwilling many* also occupy small congregations. But, give the *unwilling many* hard words and they won't follow. Don't send them any rebukes, or corrections, or admonitions to alter their lifestyles. If it becomes inconvenient for them, they are not up to the challenge. Their convenience and the feeding of their personal desires are more important to them than the *truth-in-love*.

A true prophetic voice must give the people *both* honey and grasshoppers. False teachers and false prophets only give you honey. Think about it, Jesus devoted considerable time to articulating messages that resulted in sending people away by declaring the need for commitment as genuine disciples! Jesus' words were hard words. Most listeners didn't stick with him. They left. They opted for the path of least resistance.

In a similar manner, I choose to appeal to the *willing few* in a season in history where people still have the choice. In the future there will be many others who will join the *willing few*, however only after they've tasted great difficulties. In that day when the horses come and the people are forced to escape through the thickets (re: the symbolism of Jeremiah 12:5), they will have a hard time standing and will wish that they had been *willing* earlier in their journey.

FALSE FRIENDS & REAL ENEMIES

For many years in science, business, and ministry I have noted that, *"Success draws to oneself false friends and real enemies."* Genuine spiritual leaders don't need more followers, if in fact they're drawing the wrong kinds of followers. Be cautious of who you attract. Leaders pull a drag net behind them. A drag net sinks to the bottom of the ocean and it captures everything in its path including all kinds of fish, some edible, others not. It even collects discarded tires and worthless rusty tin cans from the ocean bottom. Some followers are edible fish, others are just rusty tin cans.

Followers can come to us as *wolves in sheep's clothing* (see Matthew 7:15-23). A cloaked enemy is a dangerous fellow. The Lord showed me spiritual dreams/visions concerning this point while in Nigeria in 2005. In the dreams, while I was sitting quietly outside a full-size gray wolf with a *dog collar* (like a clerical collar worn by priests) gently approached me. It was behaving like a calm gentle collie dog. It looked domesticated. Yet, when it came next to me I declare, *"But you're a wolf!"* as I struck it on the head with my fist. It scampered away, waited a little while for another opportunity. The wolf circled back once more. When it approached me the second time, I repeated, *"But you're a wolf!"* and struck it again on the head, causing it to leave for good. The immediate application of this dream/vision was to be warned in advance about a minister I was to soon encounter. He was a cleric in view of the dog collar symbolism, and the Spirit indicated that although he appeared domesticated and gentle, he was in fact a dangerous false teacher. I also "saw" that women following this minister idolized him and that he was attracted to money. I did in fact encounter this minister and the women in his entourage did idolize him. What had been shown in the dreams became reality. I saw it play out with my own eyes.

The devil is effective at this wolf-in-sheep's-clothing strategy. It is in his very nature to be a deceiver. He is the father of lies. Should it surprise us that many of his deceived and deceiving followers seek to infiltrate the ranks of the Church? The devil wants to plant within local churches all kinds of counterfeits and deceivers, and many of them clamor for leadership roles.

Don't be surprised as you ascend in leadership responsibility to encounter both groups of individuals, *false friends* and *real enemies*. If you're not involved in "leadership", then few will likely want to follow you anyway. I'm still in the process of learning to be more discerning of peoples' motives when they approach me. It is not always what it appears to be on the surface. As an example, *passive-aggressive* individuals will smile, shake your hand, and say words of honor and flattery to your face. Then, they'll walk away and talk behind your back with all kinds of derogatory accusations. Friends, if you desire to be a leader in front, don't be surprised if people talk behind your back! Think about it…it's unavoidable.

Some folks seem to be friendly to your face, but in fact are *bona fide* "false friends". Some will seek to manipulate you or to use your reputation and network of colleagues and your endorsements of them for their own gain. They might seek your anointed blessings of their lives. Their *tools* include flattery, encouragement, favors, and inserting themselves in some manner to be associated with you or your name. Some of them exhibit pride, secret envy at your successes, or just desire an opportunity to "coat tail" on your anointing. Some may seek to obtain private information from you for their own passive-aggressive agendas. Be careful of crafty people who do this and especially those who ask you to join with them in a "covenant" relationship. Don't do it!

In addition, pay close attention to your long-term trusted "inner core" friends, who have the spiritual gifts of discernment and wisdom. These true discerning friends can help you identify the motives of the false friends who are seeking an entry point into your life or ministry. If you don't have a discerner in your life, then find one.

Then, there are those who are "real enemies". They may exhibit bold-faced envy, anger, hostility, opposition, and slander. However, the Lord's bondservant must not be quarrelsome. And, remember that our God is an avenger of the righteous. There is one advantage to real enemies over false friends…it is easier to spot real enemies.

AFTER YOU HAVE A FOLLOWING

After a person has been recognized publicly as a "leader" they will often have a *following*. Some leaders choose to remain in obscurity, with few followers. In 2005 I attended a National Honor Society ceremony at Vestavia Hills High School at which my daughter Jeannette was chosen for membership. I was particularly struck by the message on the topic of "leadership" presented by Cha-Cha Chen, a 12th grader. A portion of her presentation stated:

In Tiananmen Square on June 5, 1989, one man's action alerted the world's attention. Identified only as the "Unknown Rebel", this unexpected, un-assuming, and undaunted figure halted before a line of seventeen Chinese army tanks, using his only weapon – his humanity... The Unknown Rebel symbolized many qualities – justice, courage, and especially leadership – as he became the face of a million-man rally for democracy. As this unnamed hero showed, leadership does not require elected positions, high titles, or world renown. Leadership requires responsibility. It requires initiative. It requires courage. Above all, leadership requires action. The Unknown Rebel exemplified leadership by taking that risky step before the tanks. He epitomized leadership by showing courage despite fear. And, he symbolized leadership by inspiring others to follow him in his worthy cause.

Having previously meditated upon this overlooked or suppressed attribute of leadership, I was particularly struck that day in the high school's auditorium. Out of the articulate mouth of a high school student came a profound confirmation of what the Holy Spirit had been revealing to me. Miss Chen aptly noted the hallmarks of leadership are *responsibility, initiative, courage, and action*. Well stated! Few would doubt that this lone anonymous young fellow in front of the advancing army tanks was not a leader, in the truest sense of the term. Yet, he was just one man doing as he was inspired. None stood behind or beside him. His courage that day before the tanks and before the eyes of millions of TV viewers said one thing…this man is a courageous leader.

There are plenty of so-called leaders who have followers, yet they fail to demonstrate these critical defining virtues. To my way of understanding they are not leaders, they are pseudo-leaders. Sure they may have a following, just as Jesus spoke of the blind leading the blind. Will they not both fall into a pit? By analogy, there are both true and false ministers who each perform roles as moralistic spokesmen, yet only one of them follows the rules of righteousness. If a so-called spiritual leader fails to demonstrate *responsibility, initiative, courage, and action* (e.g., obedience), then they don't deserve to have followers. In view of this perspective on assessing genuine spiritual leaders, don't be quick to judge someone based solely on the numbers of followers. You could have many followers and yet be a poor spiritual leader. Alternatively you could have a handful of followers, but because you are playing by the righteous rules of the Kingdom, you are a better leader than the individual who has a large entourage following him or her. Let us put to rest the myth that the numbers of followers is *the* metric for leaders.

There is a trap for equating leadership with the size of the group following the leader. It is the snare of the *fear of man*. Many so-called leaders attract to themselves followers for the wrong reasons. These so-called leaders desire the accolades, influence, income, elevation, and in some cases idol worship for themselves. And, once they have amassed a following, they are reluctant to say anything to offend those who follow them. They are more focused on the numbers than on the *fear of the Lord*. Think about it! The fear of man is the opposite of the fear of the Lord. You cannot serve two masters. If you desire to have people "like" you, then you will compromise essential truths and be a poor leader, even if you can attract large audiences. A true leader will speak the truth when she or he is prompted by the Holy Spirit to do so, even if the consequences offend some of the followers. A pseudo-leader will not offend his or her "base". This person will do anything to maximize the numbers.

COUNT THE COST, THEN FOLLOW

A careful survey of Jesus' teachings on the Kingdom of God in the Gospels shows a surprising attitude toward gathering followers. Jesus discouraged many people from following Him! He maximized time with Peter, James, and John in His inner circle. He had the twelve apostles in the next layer of the onion, plus some trusted women like the sisters of Lazarus, Martha and Mary, and also Mary Magdalene.

But, Jesus was not keen on gathering people to himself, *unless* they would deny themselves, pick up their own crosses, and follow him. It was always conditional. Jesus was such a radical that He wanted his followers to be prepared for martyrdom if necessary (see Matthew 10:38). To be a "witness" is synonymous with being a "martyr" in the Greek. Jesus was not keen on gathering people to Himself, *unless* they would demonstrate love to Him by obeying Him. Didn't He question potential followers with, *"Why do you call me 'Lord, Lord', and not do what I say?"* (Luke 6:46). He is either your "Lord", meaning *boss*, or He isn't. You just can't slice the cake any other way. He's Lord or He is not. That is the test of whether you are a *disciple* or something less.

Furthermore, Jesus was not keen on gathering people to Himself, *unless* they would count the cost of building the correct foundation (see Luke 14:28-30). Jesus was not keen on gathering people to Himself, *unless* they would give up everything to follow Him (see Luke 14:31-33). And, Jesus was not keen on gathering people to Himself, *unless* they repented of their sins. Unfortunately repentance is largely a forgotten truth in Western "churchianity" today. I thank God that in many other nations this "key" discipline is alive and well. Repentance is the true on-ramp to the Highway of the Lord. Without repentance we would be disqualified from participating in the Kingdom of God.

Jesus didn't want mere believers who have mere mental assent to the truth. He wanted followers who would be repentant disciples. He wanted those who knew it would cost them heavily to follow Him. He wanted those who would be obedient, repentant, and servants in His righteous, holy, hell-shaking Kingdom! He's building a spiritual army, not a democracy. That army will become increasingly effective at re-claiming lost territory. So-called believers, who aren't obedient to Him, are of limited value in His army. They are easy cannon fodder for the enemy.

He proclaimed that He desired to bring fire to the earth, and He earnestly desired for it to be kindled into a blazing flame. Fire speaks of cleansing, purging, and judgment. In Matthew chapter 10, Jesus declared, *"Do not suppose that I have come to bring peace to the earth. I did not come to bring peace, but a sword."* (Matthew 10:34). He continues in that passage to say the result of following Him will be great division among the members of a family (i.e., between disciples and non-disciples). Jesus further drives the point home to full effect, *"Anyone who loves his father or mother more than me is not worthy of me; anyone who loves his son or daughter more than me is not worthy of me, and anyone who does not take his cross and follow me is not worthy of me. Whoever finds his life will lose it, and whoever loses his life for my sake will find it."* (Matthew 10:37-39). Jesus meant what he said! Let's not sugarcoat the truth, by denying the obvious explicit meaning.

In Luke chapter 14 we discover a parallel to these harsh words from another writer's perspective, but Jesus says if you don't do what He's saying to do, then you are disqualified from becoming His disciple. Millions of Westerners regularly attend churches, yet I would characterize their love for themselves, their spouses, or their children as being higher in priority than their love of Jesus. Yet, they still claim to be His disciples. Are they? Or, are they ignorant of Jesus' own words? Many of His words are not pleasant. They are not sweetened to make them *seeker-targeted* and more appealing. His words are extremely provocative, blunt, and piercing of the heart.

Friends, think about it. Jesus essentially drew a line in the sand and asked the crowds, *"Are you in, or are you out?"* He didn't make it easy to follow Him. Yes, this is the same Jesus that we hear so often referred to as the loving Jesus of the New Covenant, of the New Testament, and of the "new" era of *grace.* Unless we play by His rules, we're just plain deceived. Lets pray that today's ministers, who are so enamored with the idea of numerical growth for growth's sake, would see the folly of "more is better...bigger is better...and just show-me-the-money". We must be awakened to this reality in a new way.

My primary concern in this chapter is to encourage the myriads of leaders-in-training and leaders with few followers at present. They need to find hope in the midst of their current circumstances, and not be falsely labeled as a "non-leader" because of this misleading single metric of *"in order to be a leader one must have followers".* Let's move beyond this limiting myth, and embrace the diversity of expressions of Biblical leadership. Let's affirm and build up the hope of those aspiring to accomplish great things for a great God, even when few are following.

9
TEN STEPS TO RECOVER HOPE

If you or a friend of yours is currently captive to hopelessness, here are ten practical steps to help regain hope. Most of the suggestions will not cost any money. But, you or your friend will need to take some action:

#1 – TALK TO A FRIEND

Conversation is therapeutic and helps bring clarity during times of confusion. Relationships provide encouragement, affirmation, rebukes, and other beneficial outcomes. Often others can see our situations from a more objective point of view. *"Two are better than one, because they have a good return on their work: If one falls down, his friend can help him up. But pity the man who falls and has no one to help him up!"* (Ecclesiastes 4:9-10). So, seek out a friend who can bring a listening ear, or a hug, or encouragement, or some trusted counsel into the situation. A wise friend might also have a greater measure of faith for us that we lack at that moment of need.

#2 – LAUGH

It will likely seem to be one of the most ridiculous notions at the moment while experiencing hopelessness, but laughter has the power to alter the mind and the spirit realm. My good friend Howard Morgan is a talented Bible teacher. He has encountered plenty of criticism and spiritual attacks, in large part because he is a Jewish man who embraced Jesus (Yeshua) as the Messiah. Through that one action he and his family incurred significant hostilities. Yet, Howard often quips when someone is under the gun of attack to just laugh in response. Laughter is an effective tool in spiritual warfare. Laughter is an evidence that you have not lost your position of hope, and that you remain secure assured of the sovereign hand of the Almighty. Joy is an evidence of anticipated victory. The comedian Bill Cosby declared, *"Through humor, you can soften some of the worst blows that life delivers. And once you find laughter, no matter how painful your situation might be, you can survive it."* Laughter pushes hopelessness aside. Laughter minimizes the downside. Laughter celebrates the moment. It opens the door for gratitude, and is an evidence of contentment. *"A cheerful heart is good medicine…"* (Proverbs 17:22a).

#3 – ASSIST SOMEONE WHO IS WORSE OFF

Get your focus off of yourself. Shift into altruism. The Spirit once prompted me to practical action with, *"Meet others' needs before your wants!"* Life's difficulties and obstacles are relative; there are differing levels of adversity. When we shift our minds from our own concerns to those around us, from our *wants* to their *needs*, we walk in the light of the Kingdom (see Matthew 6). As we meet others' needs, He meets our needs. Our task is to obey His counsel, not to pursue our own path of comfort.

#4 – GET OUT OF BED

Depression gives birth to various emotions and it produces lethargy. That lazy withdrawn disposition in turn gives birth to more depression. Depression leads to too much rest, which in turn leads to more depression. It is a vicious cycle. *"A little sleep, a little slumber, a little folding of the hands to rest – and poverty will come on you like a bandit and scarcity like an armed man."* (Proverbs 6:10). Stop focusing on how you *feel!* The answer can be simple…Get out of bed!

#5 – DEVELOP AN ETERNAL PERSPECTIVE

The devil wants us to "buy now and pay later". Let's flip it around for the proper Kingdom perspective. Let's consider the cost today for an eternity spent with the consequences of our choices. Permit the reality and glory of heaven to invade your world today. You only have one life to invest in the Kingdom, and it restarts each day. Forgetting what lies behind, press on to the future.

"The Spirit himself testifies with our spirit that we are God's children. Now if we are children, then we are heirs—heirs of God and co-heirs with Christ, if indeed we share in his sufferings in order that we may also share in his glory. I consider that our present sufferings are not worth comparing with the glory that will be revealed in us. The creation waits in eager expectation for the sons of God to be revealed. For the creation was subjected to frustration, not by its own choice, but by the will of the one who subjected it, in hope that the creation itself will be liberated from its bondage to decay and brought into the glorious freedom of the children of God. We know that the whole creation has been groaning as in the pains of childbirth right up to the present time. Not only so, but we ourselves, who have the first fruits of the Spirit, groan inwardly as we wait eagerly for our adoption as sons, the redemption of our bodies. For in this hope we were saved. But hope that is seen is no hope at all. Who hopes for what he already has? But if we hope for what we do not yet have, we wait for it patiently." (Romans 8:16-25). Later in this same chapter we read that *all things* work together for the good of those who are called according to His purposes. From the eternal perspective, all things do work out according to God's sovereign plan.

#6 – GIVE THANKS

Gratitude lifts the heart. It blesses the recipient as well as the one speaking the words. It is more blessed to give than to receive. In all circumstances we're to give thanks. (1 Thessalonians 5:18). Thanksgiving and praise for the Almighty are powerful weapons in the Kingdom of God.

#7 – CONFESS YOUR SIN

Many of us are enslaved by sin patterns. We need to be freed from the consequences of sin. Confess your sins to one another. After repentance (i.e., changing our minds and actions), times of refreshing can come (see James 5:16 and Proverbs 28:13). As we walk in the light we'll have fellowship with one another and the blood of Jesus will cleanse us from all of our sins.

#8 – GIVE A GIFT TO SOMEONE

"A generous man will prosper; he who refreshes others will himself be refreshed." (Proverbs 11:25). Build up your account by giving away. Jesus said he who gives up everything for the sake of the Kingdom will gain his life. Giving is a part of God's character, and anyone who is in relationship with the Lord will in turn become a giver. The story of Mephibosheth is a delightful account of restoring hope to a hopeless man. He was the crippled son of David's former close friend, Jonathan. King David honored Mephibosheth late in life with an unexpected gift. David rescued him from hopelessness and elevated him once again to the King's table. Through David's intentional generosity Mephibosheth's family's possessions were restored. This is an encouraging story of how loyalty, love, and generosity can restore hope to the hopeless (see 1 Samuel 19-20 and 2 Samuel 9).

#9 – SING AND DANCE

Make a joyful noise unto the Lord. Listen to worship music. Come before His presence with singing. Bless His holy Name. Let your liver, lungs, muscles, bones, and kidneys praise Him. We should loosen the shackles of the *spirit of religion* holding us back like the *Frozen Chosen*. We should celebrate with our whole being, not just our mind. We are commanded to love the Lord our God will all of our *body*, soul, and spirit. King David danced passionately with child-like abandon before the Ark of the Covenant on its homeward journey (see 2 Samuel 6). He wholeheartedly used all of his physical body, his emotions and thoughts (the soul), and his spirit. If it is good enough for King David, shouldn't it be good enough for us?

#10 – ESTABLISH A GOAL FOR YOUR LIFE

Give yourself a reason to live that is higher than yourself, and requires the hand of God to overcome your weakness. If you reach for the stars you might actually conquer the fear of heights or learn how to fly. Goals give added meaning to life. *"Delight yourself in the Lord and he will give you the desires of your heart."* (Psalm 37:4). He did not send us to the earth to merely survive in mediocrity and to pay our bills. He sent us here as His ambassadors (2 Corinthians 5:20), as His soldiers, and His servants. He granted us breath so that our being could be used to magnify His greatness throughout the earth. Pursue a lofty goal that requires faith to be realized.

Any one of these ten steps is a minor thing, and likely free or inexpensive. Yet, it could be the source of renewal of hope in your life. It could be the first step in breaking the stranglehold of hopelessness. Take a small step on that journey!

OBEDIENCE – JUST DO SOMETHING!

In 1792, William Carey, a Particular Baptist from Moulton, England wrote a fascinating booklet. He was one of the "Dissenters", those disciples of Jesus who separated from the established government-sanctioned Church of England. In his small book he detailed a call to action for world evangelism entitled, <u>An Enquiry into the Obligations of Christians, to Use Means for the Conversion of the Heathens, in Which the Religious State of the Different Nations of the World, the Success of Former Undertakings, and the Practicability of Further Undertakings, are Considered</u>. Nowadays we would call that book title alone a "mouthful" or a "book" in itself!

I've taken friends to the thatched-roof village of Moulton a couple of times. We went to honor this great British Man of Faith. While there we absorb some of the carpet fibers from the chapel where he preached, while we laid prostrate in prayer. Carey showed an extreme level of hope about the future and God's call upon his life. He was likely the most influential path clearer for the Gospel in India and he was later honored as the *Father of Modern Missions*. His accomplishments while in India came at a great cost to his family. He was a champion of the Great Commission.

While meditating on the Great Commission spelled out so succinctly at the end of Matthew chapter 28, I noticed a new subtle emphasis, at least for me. This Scripture says in essence:

- **Go**…Get up and go; leave your home and reach outward.
- **Make Disciples**…In your "going" make *disciples* of all the nations (literally the different ethnos people groups). Notice it doesn't say to make *believers*.
- **Baptize**…Immerse the disciples in the presence and power of the Trinity (and/or immerse them underwater as a symbol of repentance and cleansing of sin).
- **Teach**…The disciples are to be taught to obey all that Jesus commanded.

What really caught my attention was that it didn't say merely "teach them" or "teach them the Scriptures". Rather, it says to teach them **to obey all that Jesus commanded**. Jesus gave his disciples expectations and requirements, and He meant for them to do all that He had commanded. He didn't stop with the admonishment to merely teach. His instruction also included the much more difficult standard of imputing to his "deputies" to make sure that the believers *obeyed* as disciples. Jesus said, *"If they obeyed my teaching, they will obey yours also."* (John 15:20b).

In the West, we've had nearly 1700 years of "church" experiences containing teachings that just fill the mind. Our Western heads are full of teaching and knowledge…lots of knowledge and little wisdom. We need teachings that impact the heart, stirring us to obedience, not merely gathering head knowledge of theology.

Obedience separates the men from the boys. Obedience is the true test of a disciple of Christ. Belief can be easy for a believer, but obedience is another thing altogether. It is one thing to merely teach, it is another to admonish and exhort people to action in obedience.

We are stirred in our emotions by certain songs. They put a fresh coat of optimistic paint over an otherwise negative situation. Music lifts the spirit, a fact demonstrated by David as a minstrel before an angry King Saul. Music can soothe the soul or motivate toward action. The lyrics of Lee Ann Womack's country song *I Hope You Dance* capture well this call to action:

I hope you never lose your sense of wonder
You get your fill to eat, but always keep that hunger
May you never take one single breath for granted
God forbid love ever leave you empty handed
I hope you still feel small, when you stand by the ocean
Whenever one door closes, I hope one more opens

[Chorus] Promise me you'll give faith a fighting chance
And when you get the choice to sit it out or dance
I hope you dance
I hope you dance

I hope you never fear those mountains in the distance
Never settle for the path of least resistance
Living might mean taking chances, but they're worth taking
Lovin' might be a mistake, but it's worth making
Don't let some hell bent heart leave you bitter
When you come close to selling out, reconsider
Give the heavens above more than just a passing glance

PART II
SOLICITED CONTRIBUTION

In order to provide the reader with a confirmatory "Amen" to what has been already presented, I requested that my trusted bi-vocational friend and colleague in ministry, John Manwell, provide his own insights on the topic of hope. John is a man of wisdom, encouragement, and prophetic awareness. He oversees an Isaiah 58 type of pastoral and apostolic-prophetic ministry in a huge home in Liverpool, England that is used to host ministers of the Gospel from the nations. He and his wife, Marie, routinely breathe hope into the despairing, who are invited into their home as they "lick their wounds" and make preparations to "get back in the saddle". I therefore thought John's brief comments would be more valuable as a confirmatory chapter, rather than as a Foreword to this project. I chose to *not* share any drafts of this book with him, so as to not bias his views on this important topic. Neither did I tailor any of my comments based upon what John had written in this solicited chapter, when I was finalizing the draft of the book. There are many striking similarities and themes to John's perspectives on hope that are recorded elsewhere in this book. Enjoy my colleague's insights on the critical virtue of hope!

10
HOPE THAT MAKES
A REAL DIFFERENCE

BY JOHN MANWELL

A short walk from our home in Liverpool is a cemetery where the inscriptions on a gravestone caught my attention:

> In *loving memory of Margaret Evans*
> *Loving wife of Bill and devoted mother of Ted*
> *Who fell asleep 6ᵗʰ July 1985 aged 60 years*
> **"To find eternal peace with our Lord**
> **O for one wish: To turn back the clock and reveal our true**
> **feelings"**
>
> *Bill Evans*
> *Husband of Margaret, father and good friend of Ted*
> *Who fell asleep 22ⁿᵈ September 1988 aged 69 years*
> **"Resting peacefully**
> **The clock has turned"**

This seems to encapsulate the essence of all that is *true* about authentic Biblical hope, and at the same time, all that can be utterly deceptive about *false* hope that is so often offered in this life. The inscription captures the poignancy of the pain that families can realize in death: Not only the loss of a loved one, but also the loss of the opportunity to let that loved one know just how they had been valued. This brings a desperate desire to have another chance to meet again and to put things right.

If the inscription was written in the genuine knowledge that these two were believers in Jesus Christ with a *real* hope of being reunited in the next life, then this is real hope. If believers, Bill and Margaret are now reunited in everlasting peace, and Bill has that opportunity to 'turn back the clock' and let Margaret know his true affection for her.

If the inscription is a vain effort to mask the pain that was felt when loved ones passed away, then it was *counterfeit* hope. If they were not right with God, then they are far from resting eternally and recovering old losses, but separate and suffering eternal unending anguish. We need to know the difference between these two opposites.

Hope is not wishful thinking, but a basis of expectation of the reality that lies ahead. Genuine hope makes a tangible and real difference. Real hope stimulates faith into life and feeds it. False hope feeds the emotions, and is temporary, ultimately disappointing. Hope raises the heart, and the opposite, when hope is deferred, it makes the heart sick (see Proverbs 13:12). Hope is intimately related to *faith*, as we all know from Hebrews 11:1, and we must study hope in this context.

There is a worldly view of hope that is closely related to a 'lottery mentality'. This is captured in the phrase "hoping for the best". It is a wishful thinking that is a mixture of delusion, escapism and is unrealistic. A lack of hope is an absence of a way ahead; a complete lack of avenues to progress. The way the world has taught many people to seek hope is to simply wish for something better, and to dream of wonderful changes or great provision to fall upon them.

Life without hope is a struggle in which most things are negative or bring negative thoughts to mind. Every illness and event presents a possibility of terminal illness or catastrophe. Hope cuts off this pattern of thinking and draws a line on this way of viewing life and believing.

Once hope arrives, the number of options and positive possibilities opens up almost without limit. The person who is living in hope and thinking with an attitude of hope is making available an unending number of areas to explore. Hope brings a mindset that opens up tremendous variety and creative solutions to all challenges. A lack of hope closes possibilities down and reduces the horizon down to the immediate and impossible.

There is a wonderful insight into what hope does for us in the book of Proverbs:

> *Eat honey, my son, for it is good;*
> *Honey from the comb is sweet to your taste.*
> *Know also that wisdom is sweet to your soul;*
> *If you find it, there is a future hope for you,*
> *And your hope will not be cut off.* (Proverbs 24:13-14)

I love these short verses. In a few words this captures the sweetness of receiving wisdom for life, and how in doing so, we increase in hope and our future is opened up instead of being cut down.

When God began the process of creation there lay ahead a truly immense and wonderful diversity of materials, colors, actions, movements, living beings, varied lives and events. We know that God created the earth and heavens by faith and His spoken Word. We should also reflect on the fact that as He was creating everything, He KNEW for certain what lay ahead. God created the cosmos with a perfect sense of hope for what was coming. Put another way, God was not wishfully longing for the things that lay ahead, but that being God, He was outside of the constraint of time and *knew as a fact* everything about the end from the beginning. I would say that this is what true hope is based on. Godly and Biblical hope is rooted in certain knowledge and a solid expectation rather than uncertain wishful thinking.

In every area of human life there is great value in working, planning, thinking and imagining within a framework of hope. A mentality of hope enables us in anything we care to think of, whether scientific research, politics or social planning or any everyday area of family life and work.

Let's consider several areas of life as we know it and how hope impacts upon them: At the basic level of individual motivation, men are fundamentally driven towards action and the hope of success. They know that certain actions produce results, and are driven by the desire to achieve desirable outcomes. Women are drawn towards relationships and knowing each other more. They know that getting to know people is rewarding and keeps friendships and families together and healthy. They are both urged on by the hope of the outcome they want. Healthy families are the basis of hope for our society.

Let's look at society and what it is based on: Our western society, particularly in Britain and America was based on the hope of the Kingdom of God. That is to say that our laws, judicial system and principles of business started out from Biblical precepts, and are built on the clear understanding that obeying God and submitting to His truth results in healthy society and consequent peace and prosperity. This is another way of saying that living God's way is to live in the hope that obeying his principles will bring about His pleasure and we will all benefit from His blessing.

For many generations Christian society and culture were based on a hope in the afterlife resulting from obeying God in this life. The Christian message offers blessing in this life, but the over-riding goal is our hope in the everlasting world to come. This hope is steadfast and certain, and provides a solid bed-rock for our society and institutions in family, education and the business world. This is a hope that permeates every aspect of life and thinking in our culture and daily living. Our hope in God and hope of eternal life motivates us to live well and to do good. In this way hope is the engine and power for a strong and stable society. Living God's way does not just open up a possibility, a chance that things will work well, but a certain and definite commitment from God.

In this generation we are seeing a new kind of hope being offered. This is a false and temporal hope. People are being seduced across the world with hope of becoming rich and hope of being lucky in life. The infection of false hope is seen in every walk of life. We are hypnotised with the wafer thin 'hope' of winning the lottery and becoming super-rich in a day. Many hard working families long for the day that they might have a dream holiday or afford a luxury car or enviable home. The essence of the hope the world is offering is short term, wishful thinking, luck based, and faintly possible. It usually requires someone else to suffer less good fortune to make it possible. The very concept of a lottery is a deception that rakes in millions of dollars from millions of people who cannot afford to throw money away. They are given a fleeting taste of what feels like 'hope' in return for wasting their money on the smallest probability of winning.

The book of Proverbs says that money quickly gained is soon lost.

Modern thinkers want us to be raised with the random and impersonal concept of evolution as being the way in which we all came into being. We are fed on the belief in democracy and the *rightness* of the majority. All of this conditions us to think in terms of possibilities and probabilities and 'luck' as the route through to good fortune and positive outcomes. Little wonder that we easily adopt the world view of hope as a sense of *"things might get better, if we could only close our eyes and dream a little longer or a little harder!"* Most drug abuse and alcoholism is a result of people in pain wanting a sense of hope. But, they get a counterfeit, a feeling of positive elation that can be bought for a moment.

Hope in God is certain and defined, making for a solid and consistent society. Hope in *luck* is vague and relativistic, without a reference point and is drifting. Hope in luck will ultimately lead to social collapse and possibly violent hatred, as people turn on each other with nothing real or eternal to look forward to. The Bible warns that without vision, the people perish. Vision is a form of hope.

EXAMPLES OF THE APPLICATION OF HOPE

ART

There is a whole movement of dark and hopeless art. This is justified in terms of "reflecting reality". The mood conveyed is depressing and seems to show life at its worst. This approach to 'art' projects violence, anger, decay, emptiness and insanity. When one considers all that is possible in the world, this kind of art, whether it is a painting, song, or photograph, is surely not motivating people to rise to new heights and possibilities.

An alternative is to challenge and inspire. Art can be used to provoke people to do something, and rise above the failures and disappointments. Even decay and brokenness can be conveyed in a form that challenges us to respond and do something positive. Art can be inspiring and pointing to what life can be at its best.

SCIENCE

When scientists and technologists approach their craft with a humanistic and hopeless framework, the technology and knowledge is simply a tool to control and take advantage. Technology without hope is crushing and degrades society. An example of this would be development of biological weapons, designed to kill and maim large numbers of civilians and used to create fear in the enemy population. A more mundane example would be the cynical use of modern technology that allows ordinary people to gamble on-line, spurred on by the rush of adrenalin and having their money drained from their family.

Alternatively innovation and creativity can be used to open possibilities and help people to be all they can be. Wonderful examples of this exist in medicine, such as computers that enable paralysed people to speak, or cures developed for cancers. Internet innovations that help people to track down long lost friends from school is another example of how technology can be positive in our frantic world.

When technologists are motivated with hope their energy is directed towards a goal that strengthens and helps people. Those without hope develop tools that kill, steal and destroy.

GOVERNMENT

When leaders and rulers have hope that values people and the fear of God, their approach is constructive. An example was William Wilberforce. As a God fearing politician he knew that the African slave trade was an evil that should stop. He had a hope in the Kingdom of God and a genuine hope that Godly principles could prevail. In 1791 he presented his first bill before the British Parliament attempting to outlaw the slave trade. The bill was unsuccessful, losing by 163 votes to 88. With hope in the eternal and hope in what he believed to be the right action he persevered. Year after year Wilberforce brought revised bills to the Parliament. Eventually in 1807 the bill he brought was passed by 114 votes to 15. He continued to campaign for existing slaves to be given their freedom. He died in July 1833 not having seen his passionate desire achieved. One month later the British Parliament passed a law giving all slaves in the

British Empire their freedom. This is a great example of hope motivating a leader and a cause (read the biography of Wilberforce in <u>Amazing Grace</u> by Eric Mataxas). It shows a man inspired and strengthened in his work by hope. It also reminds us that we don't always see for ourselves in this life what we hope for, but it may happen anyway.

In contrast, President Idi Amin took power in Uganda in 1971 through a military coup. His wicked rule was without compassion for his people and society. Observers estimate that he oversaw the killing of between 300,000 and 500,000 people within his country. It was said that he enjoyed killing people, and that he even killed one of his own wives. What a powerful example of a ruler without hope as a motive and certainly not giving hope to his people.

MANAGEMENT

Many of us have seen management that has no hope for eternal life and no sense of inspiration. This type of management simply uses people as resources. Staff are treated as numbers to be controlled, dominated and all outcomes are seen as dependant on human ability, and all results must be measurable in the 'here and now'. This belief system, operating within a manager, is reflected in actions that use and abuse people as they all operate within an environment of hopeless pursuit of money, material results, and temporary glory.

Conversely, many of us have experienced leaders and leadership that has an eternal hope. Leaders who have hope in their own hearts and this reflects in a hope for others. This kind of leadership has optimism about people and a wider perspective on what is achieved, and confidence in what others could be. Their hope from within is contagious.

FAMILY

We live in an age when families and family life are under attack. Those families that have hope for the future are able to grow, develop and aspire to all kinds of possibilities. Parents' marriages survive all kinds of pressures when they have hope beyond the conflict. Children see parents living in hope for what lies ahead and for a life that is more than just the present material age, and the children in turn, learn to deal with pressure and the trials of life. In this environment children grow in hope and this enables them to fulfill their potential as people, who in turn spread hope in an otherwise hopeless world. A hope-filled family demonstrates and lives in healthy leadership and security, works towards meaningful goals, and sees fulfillment in life.

Following the financial crash of 1929 there were many people who lost everything and businesses that collapsed to nothing. Yet, there were also some who began businesses that later became the biggest and most successful businesses of the century. The inner response to a dramatic change is either hope or hopelessness. Hope produces new life and opportunities, where hopelessness results in death.

We rise to what we are looking at. We need an internal view, which is hopeful. Hope produces perseverance. We need to be clear that hope is not a peripheral, secondary or sideline issue. What we hope in, and hope for, is central to who we are and how our society and culture will develop. Hope impacts on our thinking, our goals and our national life. Even our faith will be shaped and develop by the hope that we carry in the core of our being.

Hope is the road that faith walks on.

When our brains are working, the electrical impulses release neurotransmitters, which in turn reinforce the pathway for those electrical connections. Good results produce a positive pathway. In other words 'proven' positive experience creates knowledge or certainty that opens up the thinking and ability to imagine, problem solve, and deal with challenges. In a physical and practical way, our brains are literally more <u>able</u> to deal with life's challenges when positive outcomes are envisaged. This is more and more the case as positive thoughts and positive results are repeated. The inverse is true. When negative results or pain occur, the pathways are closed down and minimized. This closes down the mental capacity for fresh thinking or new solutions.

On its own this is a line of thinking that simply reduces hope to nothing more than 'positive thinking.' If this was the case, the lottery type of hope would do us good! The point is that even at a physiological level there is a practical case for having hope and nurturing a positive optimistic expectation.

At a more profound level, a correct understanding of hope as a spiritual truth can do the same for our spirit. Spiritual truth, received into each of our spirits through the written Word of God and the breathed out Spirit of God, trains our spirits in the positive and encouraging revelation of God. Our spirits become stimulated and informed. We develop and learn to have greater confidence in the resources and government of God in our lives. Our spiritual resources are increased and widened so that we are more able to deal with spiritual challenges and more effectively arrive at solutions provided by God. The opposite is true when we dull our spirits with lies from the world and the realm of darkness. Our capacity to face difficulties and defeat satanic opposition becomes ever diminishing. For these reasons we must renew our minds and not think as the world does. Training our spirits with God's Word and His thoughts will develop spiritual hope and inner resources. As we gain awareness of the hope to which we are called and the glory that lies ahead, we become confident in God and sure of the road that we are on.

Knowing God's plan for what is to come is very reassuring. It is a stronghold against all the invasions of the world and satan. We need to know what God has ordained for all humanity and every believer. We also need to know His specific plan and purpose for every one of us. Each one of us needs to be clear of His call and intention for our individual life. Knowing this and looking forward with a certain hope changes the way we will respond to the events that spring up.

An example of this from my life makes the point. At the end of 1993, after much prayer, I knew that in the year ahead (1994) God wanted me to get a new job and develop into new things. I started the year with this knowledge and I was hopeful about it! A few weeks into the year God spoke to me in a hotel room in Barcelona while I was on a business trip. He emphasized the words of Isaiah 43:19, *"See I am doing a new thing, see it now springs up."* I knew for certain that God was letting me know that he was shortly about to do a new thing. I understood that it would follow very soon after that night. Two days later when I returned to my office in England, I was called in to see my manager. He informed me that it was necessary to make my job redundant (that means to be "fired" to the Yankees).

In that moment my head spun and my heart leapt! I knew the hope of what God had already said. I was able to respond in that moment from a position of hope and deal with the situation in faith. I still had to deal with the uncomfortable emotional aspects of not being wanted by my company and of facing the prospect of not having a job. I was however, able to live with confident assurance in front of my work colleagues and to reassure and lead my family with positive and real faith. The whole transition in our lives was a testimony of faith and an example to friends and family, both believers and non-believers.

A few weeks later I was delighted to walk into a better job with better pay and prospects. Even more importantly than the material results of the situation, my wife and I were ready to be released to the next level of faith and living in the Kingdom of God. We moved on to the next stage of pursuing the hope and vision that God had given us several years before regarding our long-term calling and ministry. The hope that was planted and strong in my heart on the morning that I was made redundant was real and made a definite and actual difference in the situation and the outcome.

My favorite passage in the Bible on the subject of hope is in the book of Romans: *"I consider that our present sufferings are not worth comparing with the glory that will be revealed in us. The creation waits in eager expectation for the sons of God to be revealed. The creation was subjected to frustration, not by its own choice, but by the will of the one who subjected it, in hope that the creation itself will be liberated from its bondage to decay and brought to the glorious freedom of the children of God. We know that the whole creation has been groaning as in the pains of childbirth right up to the present time. Not only so, but we ourselves, who have the first-fruits of the Spirit, groan inwardly as we wait eagerly for our adoption as sons, the redemption of our bodies. For in this hope we were saved. But hope that is seen is no hope at all. Who hopes for what he already has? But if we hope for what we do not yet have, we wait for it patiently."* (Romans 8:18-25).

This passage is wonderfully self-explanatory, speaking of the glorious ultimate hope of our calling as sons of God. This is a hope that strengthens us through any manner of present trials or sufferings – if we will only look to, and by faith, draw from, the hope that God is holding out in front of us. This is not a small thing – this passage in Romans speaks of the whole of creation! It speaks of us as coming into son-ship; the whole of creation being liberated from decay and the final and complete freedom.

The vastness and comprehensiveness of this hope is then focused down to the walk of faith as, *"we wait for it patiently."*

God is calling out to the Church to understand the hope that He is offering. We are not walking in the dark and hoping that we will not trip over the furniture. We are walking in the light. As it says in Proverbs 4:18: *"The path of the righteous is like the first gleam of dawn, shining ever brighter till the full light of day."*

Let God flood your heart and life with light. It's not just a feeling of well-being. He wants you to see and understand, and that is what hope brings. Jesus is coming back. His return is the great hope for the world. Our resurrection in Him is our eternal hope. His completeness is the full light of day. Until then the light is shining ever brighter.

Ask God for real and definite hope. Learn from the Bible what he intends for believers to be and do. Let Him show you what the church and the Kingdom of God are all about. Allow Him to give you revelation to illuminate your personal path that He has prepared for you. Know for certain what He has called you to be and to do. Let Him speak the future into your life. Receive hope!

[This chapter was a solicited contribution by John Manwell of The Well in Liverpool, England. John is management consultant and executive coach. He also serves as a founding member of the Board of Directors of Path Clearer Inc.]

RECOMMENDED BOOKS

- *Praying Faith* – Thomas P. Dooley
- *Never Give Up* – Don Hawkins
- *The Hiding Place* – Corey ten Boom
- *Spiritual Leadership* – Henry Blackaby
- *Endurance: Shackleton's Incredible Voyage* – Alfred Lansing
- *The Interesting Narrative* – Olaudah Equiano
- *Biography of Hudson Taylor* – Vance Christie
- *William Carey, Father of Missions* – Sam Wellman
- *Biography of Rees Howells - Intercessor* – Norman Grubbs
- *Surprised by the Power of the Spirit* – Jack Deere
- *Repenters* – Peter Dugulescu
- *When Heaven Invades Earth* – Bill Johnson
- *One Church Many Tribes* – Richard Twiss
- *Living in Color* – Randy Woodley
- *The Seed of a Nation: Rediscovering America* – Darrell Fields
- *Amazing Grace* – Eric Mataxas
- *Revolution* – George Barna
- *The Case for Character* – Drayton Nabers

ABOUT THE AUTHOR

Dr. Thomas P. Dooley is the Founder and President of Path Clearer Inc., a ministry involved in *Influencing Nations with Judeo-Christian Truth*. He is a prophetic preacher among the nations, and the author of ***Praying Faith*** (Destiny Image Publishers). Tom has a diverse professional background and has been active in various ministries. He was a farm boy, who subsequently became a research scientist and entrepreneur. Tom has a Ph.D. in molecular biology and has worked in the pharmaceutical industry and in academia. Furthermore, Dr. Dooley is a serial entrepreneur, having founded various scientific companies and nonprofit organizations. He is an advocate for bi-vocational ministry in the marketplace and advancing the Kingdom of God outside of the local church. Dr. Dooley has a diverse set of perspectives seldom provided by other authors. He addresses the issues of *hope* and *hopelessness* from Biblical perspectives and powerful firsthand testimonies as one accustomed to living a life of faith, or risk-taking belief in action.

Tom has been married for more than a quarter century to his kind and discerning wife, Laura. They have four delightful children. The Dooley family resides near Birmingham, Alabama.

CONTACT THE AUTHOR

info@pathclearer.com
www.pathclearer.com
www.tomdooley.org

Path Clearer, Inc.
PO Box 661466
Birmingham, Alabama
35266-1466 USA